A PASTOR TO PASTOR BOOK

THE HEART

OF A GREAT

PASTOR

HOW TO GROW STRONG

AND THRIVE WHEREVER

GOD HAS PLANTED YOU

H.B. LONDON JR.
NEIL B. WISEMAN

Regal

A Division of Gospel Light
Ventura, California, U.S.A.

Regal Books
A Division of Gospel Light
Ventura, California, U.S.A.
Printed in U.S.A.

Library of Congress Cataloging-in-Publication Data
London, H. B.
    The heart of a great pastor : making the most of the unique opportunities that
can only be found where God has planted you / H.B. London, Jr., Neil B. Wiseman.
        p. cm.
    Includes bibliographical references.
    ISBN 0-8307-1689-0 (trade)
    1. Clergy—Office. 2. Pastoral theology. 3. Evangelicalism.
    I. Wiseman, Neil B. II. Title.
    BV660.2.L66 1994   94-12657
    253—dc20   CIP

10 11 12 13 14 15 / 00

Rights for publishing this book in other languages are contracted by Gospel
Literature International (GLINT). GLINT also provides technical help for the adap-
tation, translation and publishing of Bible study resources and books in scores of
languages worldwide. For further information, contact GLINT, P.O. Box 4060,
Ontario, CA 91761-1003, U.S.A., or the publisher.

For pastors everywhere

*The world and the Church await the achievement of the
dreams you dare to dream and the miracles your reenergized
ministry will bring.*

Contents

Meet
H. B. London Jr.
and
Neil B. Wiseman

H. B. London Jr. is vice president of ministry outreach and pastoral ministries at Focus on the Family in Colorado Springs, Colorado. In that assignment, H. B. is founder and director of the Pastor to Pastor ministry and is committed to encouraging and enabling pastors everywhere. Before beginning this ministry to pastors and their families at Focus on the Family, H. B. served various-size pastorates for 31 years. His most recent pastorate was a 3,100-member congregation in Pasadena, California.

H. B. often has been involved in specialized assignments in pastoral training, evangelism, overseas mission development and revivals. His present ministry to pastors through Focus on the Family includes a whirlwind conference-speaking schedule, media resource development, and counseling with pastors by phone, mail and writing. A burned-out pastor recently described the spirit of H. B.'s ministry: "Though I don't know H. B. London personally, I feel like I have a friendly listener at Focus on the Family. What a relief to know someone understands my stresses and is trying to do something about them."

H. B.'s priorities for helping pastors show in a repeated theme in his correspondence: "What happens to you matters to me."

Neil B. Wiseman, a 20-year veteran pastor, now multiplies his ministry by training pastors for the new century. As pastoral development professor at Nazarene Bible College in Colorado Springs, he teaches preaching and pastoral skills to second-career adult students. Earlier he served as college chaplain at Trevecca College in Nashville, Tennessee, and as continuing education director for his denomination.

Outside the classroom, Neil directs the Small Church Institute and edits a quarterly journal on church growth, evangelism and discipleship called GROW. He has written and/or edited more than 10 books, including *Spirituality—God's Prescription for Stress.* He also serves as a resource person for several pastoral conferences each year and preaches at local churches and conferences. Earlier, he was the academic dean at Nazarene Bible College for eight years, where he led the faculty to implement a professional undergraduate education for pastors. He is involved in developing seminars, print and audio resources for pastors and laity; he was also the founder of *Christianity Today*'s monthly sermon cassette series, "Preaching Today."

Neil describes himself as giving his ministry to pastoral potential development. That devotion shows in the phrase he uses in correspondence with pastors and former students: "Let's trade prayers."

H. B. London Jr. and Neil B. Wiseman coauthored *Pastors at Risk: Help for Pastors and Hope for the Church* in 1993. Future books are planned to praise and to encourage pastors' wives, to refocus the laity's understanding of pastors and to help congregations become extended families.

PREFACE

An Affirming Word to Our Reader Friends

Tough times call for heroic action by great souls. That is why this book was written: to help pastors renew their sense of self-worth and to revive their passion for ministry. This book praises pastors and encourages them to dream new dreams, impossible dreams.

As the authors, we believe that pastors are indispensable for society and for the Church. We appreciate what every pastor does for the Kingdom. We also want to challenge pastors to realize that they are part of society's best spiritual hope for the remainder of this decade and beyond. We believe every pastor can bloom in the holy ground where God has planted him.

About the Title
The Heart of a Great Pastor salutes pastors everywhere. The title also seeks to encourage pastors who are well on their way to greatness, the way God counts it. The potential of marshaling an army of active-duty pastors throughout the world astounds us. Think of what we can accomplish together.

This magnificent righteous army could revolutionize the spiritual core of the nation and the world. In a time of moral hand-wringing and socially confused institutions, we must not allow ourselves to forget that a network of individual actions is what most affects any society and any church. Let's make the most of the unique opportunities in the place where God has planted us.

Pastors with Great Hearts
Pastors, we believe that you are great for many reasons. Start with your abiding desire to make a difference in the world. Think of the size of this pastoral army—more than 375,000 strong in the United States alone. Think of the incredible amount of good pastors accomplish every day.

Your faithfulness, sacrifice, tenacity, courage, hard work and compassion impact the world in immeasurable ways. You are great because of your loyalty to your Commanding General. His empowerment enables you to achieve spiritual accomplishments that really matter to Him and to our world.

Today's crises cry out for this shared greatness to be poured out in winning sacrificial service that leads people to Christ, that builds solid churches and that redeems society. Our challenges and problems reach in two directions—to the Church and to the culture.

The Church Needs Great Pastors
Today, the Church of Jesus Christ finds herself caught in a crippling identity crisis, and ministers catch the brunt of it. History offers the Church no guidance because such cataclysmic changes have never occurred. Hence, an enormous upheaval in church life is happening everywhere.

Society Needs Great Pastors
In society, a coarse, moral civil war is shredding values, goodness and righteousness. As a result, dysfunction, violence and alienation have denigrated our families, schools, communities and governments. We cannot minimize the depth of this moral decay, nor the difficulty of transforming it. But reformation and revival have to come, and God promises to help us.

Ministry in the best and in the worst of times offers unprecedented opportunities even as it causes tyrannizing trauma. Although the problems appear tougher than ever before, the prospects never looked brighter.

The needs are monumental. Anyone who cannot be stirred by the conditions facing us has forgotten the amazing power of the gospel or is too
battle weary to realize what winning the war could mean to our cause.

Why This Book Was Written
Our purpose in writing this book is to encourage pastors to see unparal-
leled opportunities in every situation. We hope to provide a useful road
map for people who want to reenergize their ministry.

Although many pastors recognize possibilities for making ministry
work better, more pioneers are needed. This book is a back-to-basics
guide to help pastors launch new and greater explorations of effective
ministry. Although this book is expected to be of interest to all ministers,
it should be especially helpful to ministers of churches that have around
100 members and have a limited staff.

The Use of First Person
When the authors speak from personal experience, "I" is used. The
speaker in such instances is identified as H. B. or as Neil.

The Use of Masculine Pronouns
We realize that an increasing number of congregations are being led by
women (approximately 3 percent of churches are led by women), and we
do not wish to diminish or to subvert that fact in any way. But because
most of the book is directed to male pastors, we have used the masculine
pronoun.

Names Have Been Changed
In several instances, locations and names have been changed in examples
and in letters to protect the privacy of individuals. But every story is factual.

Renewing the Supernatural
With all our hearts, we believe a supernatural breakthrough may be
around the next bend or behind the next problem; thus, we ask Christ to
renew wild hope in your soul.

We challenge you to respond fully to the incredible needs for the gospel that shout from every cranny of society. Take courage, divine strength for every battle is just a prayer away. Make the promise of Jesus personally your own: "I chose you, and put you in the world to bear fruit, fruit that won't spoil. As fruitbearers, whatever you ask the Father in relation to me, He gives you" (John 15:16).[1]

Sound the battle call loud enough so all can hear. Enlist the troops. Move to the front. Get ready for the toughest battle of your life. Personalize Paul's charge to Timothy as your own: "Teach believers with your life: by word, by demeanor, by love, by faith, by integrity. Stay at your post reading Scripture, giving counsel, teaching. And that special gift of ministry you were given when the leaders of the church laid hands on you and prayed—keep that dusted off and in use" (1 Tim. 4:12-14).[2]

Wonderful, miraculous results are ignited by seeing through new eyes and by dreaming new dreams more than by moving to new places. Straight ahead for the Kingdom. What matters to you, matters to us.

H. B. London Jr. and Neil B. Wiseman

Notes
1. Eugene H. Peterson, *The Message* (Colorado Springs: NavPress, 1993), p. 222.
2. Ibid., p. 442.

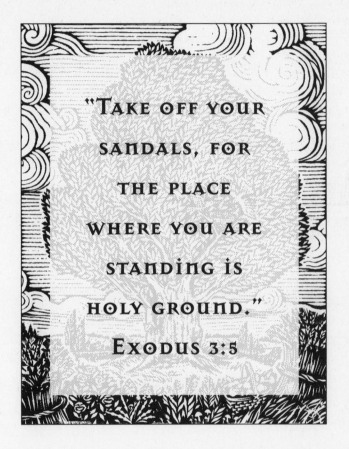

"Take off your sandals, for the place where you are standing is holy ground."

Exodus 3:5

I

EVERY ASSIGNMENT IS HOLY GROUND

Strong Lord, repot my ministry so my roots grow deep in the soil where You have planted me. Prune my efforts so the fruits are lasting and sweet. Focus my outlook so I see Your presence in every setting. Amen.

YOU'RE STANDING ON HOLY GROUND

Eight young pastors and their wives sat in front of a roaring fireplace. Any thought of venturing outdoors for some afternoon exercise was erased by a howling blizzard that swirled around their Rocky Mountain retreat.

When the conversation began to lag, Ted, much like a brash, modern-day Peter, blurted out a suggestion: "Let's make up a game in which each person describes the phase of ministry that irritates him the most."

Why-spoil-the-fun looks greeted his suggestion. He was reminded that a retreat should offer temporary sanctuary from thoughts of assignments awaiting back home. Ted's persistence prevailed, and he volunteered to start the game.

"My biggest problem," he said, "is a lay leader who is related to nearly everyone in the church. Dignified. Selfish. Hard to reach. Domineering. Desert Storm starts if anyone crosses him. So he gets his way through negative intimidation." Several heads nodded, acknowledging that Ted's experience was not unique.

Sarah, at first a bit hesitant, confessed that her husband never lets down his preacher image. "He walks, talks and thinks like a preacher. Even at home, he uses his stained-glass voice for table prayers. Romance with a reverend often isn't very exciting," she said as several participants muffled nervous laughs.

"My work is never done," was Max's discouraging frustration. "Like Los Angeles freeway traffic, it never quits. Another sermon to write. A phone call to return. Another brush fire to stomp out.

"I don't know about you," Max continued, "but money is tight every day. Some of us have thousands of dollars of college loans to pay, and the salaries of most beginners aren't big to begin with. The pressure to make ends meet never lets up."

"You're not alone," Dan responded. "My wife and I deal with discouraging financial pressure every day. We are only about $2,000 a year away from living a fairly normal life, but no one in the church seems to understand our money problem.

"Key players say absurd things like, 'God will provide.' That makes me want to scream, 'God only raises pastors' salaries through lay leaders.' I never saw dollars drop from the sky."

Grievances began to pile up as participation in the game intensified: crowded parsonages, demands on family, apathetic leaders, broken promises. As the share-the-misery therapy session progressed, a collective mood of self-pity began to brew.

Then David, tears streaming down his face, shared. "My situation is tougher than I can describe. People are brittle, demanding, unresponsive, touchy. I often want out and I complain to God.

"God sent me there, I know. And he keeps me there. He expects me to be a Christ-exalting leader there, but I wish I were somewhere else. Humanly, I want to quit."

Between sobs, David continued. "But a few good parishioners stand by me. They care about my wife and me. They care about God and His work. Even though I might want to bail out at times, I just can't leave. It's like, well, it's like I stand on holy ground."

The room grew hushed as the group of young men and women looked into the dancing fire.

"I never thought of our setting for service from that perspective," Sara said. "This discussion puts our situation in a new light and makes it sound like holy ground, too."

"Ours, too!" Tom chimed in.

"Yeah," Andy said, "I guess you could say it's that way with us. But it's the strangest holy ground I've ever seen. Sometimes it seems God has deserted the place."

During the two hours of conversation that followed, seven of the eight couples agreed that God had led them to their places of ministry, to holy ground.

The boisterous Ted, now more subdued, observed, "This conversation has caused me to think of my childhood. My mother—a pastor's wife—used to sing when times where rough, 'Where Jesus is, 'tis heaven there.'"

The words of that song and the insights gained during that Wednesday afternoon accompanied the couples as they left the Colorado conference center. They knew God was not finished with them. People still needed their ministry. And they had God's promise to empower them where they served.

Questions a Pastor Must Answer

Like the group members at the retreat, every pastor in the thick of the struggle must answer significant questions. The answers shape his ministry and determine his effectiveness:

- What difference will I make?
- Why am I here?
- Who sent me?
- Is this assignment sacred because God placed me here?
- What does God want to accomplish here?

Every assignment is holy ground because Jesus gave Himself for the people who live there. Every place is important because God wants you to accomplish something supernatural there. Every situation is special because ministry is needed there. Like Queen Esther, you have come to the Kingdom for a time like this. All of these factors give a pastor a much-needed sense of destiny about his assignment.

Think of the awesome possibilities. Your assignment may be holy ground because of a specific need in the local congregation. God may want some fresh vision or reconciliation started there. Or some outreach opportunity may await you—a neighbor to be led to Christ, a ministry to be started, a church to be refocused on biblical priorities.

Moses discovered in his lifetime that God's presence turns ministry into an adventure. As the evangelist, Luis Palau, suggests, "Any old bush will do because it is not us doing something for God, but God doing something through us."[1]

Eugene H. Peterson reminds us in his paraphrase of Scripture, *The Message*, "When you're joined with me and I with you in an intimate and organized relationship, the harvest is sure to be abundant."[2] What an extravagant promise. What amazing potential. What an unconquerable force for changing the world for Christ.

You are needed. You are important. You are empowered by God. You serve in the middle of the action. God wants to enable you to transform your present assignment into holy ground—a place where He accomplishes supernatural achievements through ordinary people.

EVERY ASSIGNMENT HAS SEVEN RESOURCES

Seven resources are available for use in every assignment, congregation and community. Although often unrecognized, these resources are never limited by geography, finances, facilities or creed. And in every church in every place, they are always available.

Resource 1: Every Congregation Is Unique
Like a family resemblance, every congregation bears a likeness to all

other churches. But each church has more distinctives than similarities, like little Tommy looks more like himself than anyone else in his family.

Consequently, using a church's uniqueness is a magnificently important factor in developing a flourishing ministry in any congregation. God gives uniqueness to a church for us to recognize and to use. Your church, like every snowflake and raindrop, has been created unlike any other.

Resource 2: Every Congregation Needs a Pastor's Love
Just as marriage partners must love each other to build a strong marriage, so a church needs to be loved by its pastor and to love its minister in

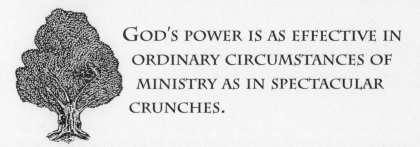

GOD'S POWER IS AS EFFECTIVE IN ORDINARY CIRCUMSTANCES OF MINISTRY AS IN SPECTACULAR CRUNCHES.

return. Pastoring a church is more like a courtship in a marriage than the process of developing a business.

Although productive pastors may employ work habits similar to those used by professional persons or business owners, they must be loving— warm, friendly and accepting. Congregations seldom thrive without a pastor's love. The sheep grow restless without an attentive shepherd.

Resource 3: God Provides Supernatural Empowerment
Contemporary sin and brokenness are not too big for God's power. He can redeem a society as easily as He created the earth. Although murder, rape, violence, white-collar crimes, abortions, divorce and unwed births sadden the heart of God, He is not paralyzed by them. If He can find a few faithful servants, He will work miracles.

Neither are complex problems in your church too big for Him. That means divine empowerment is available in every setting for every need. God's power is as effective in ordinary circumstances of ministry as in

spectacular crunches. Most churches need much more reliance on supernatural empowerments for everyday ministry. It is, after all, His church.

Resource 4: Every Church Needs Bible Preaching
God has preserved the Bible as a supernatural guide for life and faith.
Regrettably, many people consider the Bible and preaching as lifeless and
out of date. But better preaching will make every church more healthy.

The Bible, our source for preaching, needs no defense. When proclaimed in ways people understand, it always exonerates itself. Strange as
it may seem, preaching—one anointed person speaking a fresh word
from God amid the people of God—is one of the Father's favorite ways
of communicating His will to believers.

Sound scriptural preaching can help every hearer and every preacher
grow. Biblical preaching keeps molding the preacher into the image of
Christ. And for the hearers, William Willimon says it well: "People are
ripe for a voice that gives them something significant worth living and
dying for."[3]

Resource 5: Every Pastor Is Distinctively Gifted
God whispers His call for ministry to people who possess many diverse
gifts. Like snowflakes or aspen leaves, no two pastors are alike. Therefore,
the issue is: "How can I honor my call with my dedicated best in education and in personal spiritual development?"

After a wholehearted effort to personal development, a minister must
maximize his giftedness. God wants you to use His gift of originality in
every setting. Often it is surprising to see how God prepares a pastor for
a specific assignment. Our problems frustrate us when we realize we are
often called upon to use our lesser gifts rather than to refine our greater
gifts. Both are valuable and needed.

Resource 6: Every Setting Has Potential
Something special needs to be done in every setting. Somebody within
an amazingly short radius of every church needs the Savior and an
opportunity to change. It's easy to visualize needy people in East Los
Angeles or in Manhattan. Spiritually unreached people can also be found

on the next ranch in Montana, on the next farm in Missouri, on the next block in Minneapolis.

Although Kingdom opportunities usually are measured by the masses, they can only be accomplished by winning individuals who live across the fence, up the street, down the freeway or across town.

What appear to be insurmountable church problems melt like ice cubes in an August sun when we recall how many people have never heard about Christ. This might be a good time to revive the spirit of the pioneer pastor who described his work: "We went to people who did not want us and stayed until they could not get along without us."

Try this test. Check the demographics in your town. Find out how many live within easy reach but who have not discovered the hope of the Resurrection.

Resource 7: Every Church Has Something to Give People
In spite of apparent limitations, every church has something to offer in rich ministry to all who attend. It may be friendship, fellowship or restoration. Every place turns into a holy center for productive ministry when a congregation believes it has something worthwhile for every person, even to the first-time visitor.

We have been lulled into believing that the small church has little to offer. We have allowed the big-is-best mind-set to dilute the fact that when the church is the Church, it is a mighty instrument in the hand of God regardless of its size.

NEEDED: A MODERN MOSES

Ideal conditions do not create a satisfying ministry. Real meaning comes from developing an intimacy with the Lord Jesus. Accordingly, in every situation a pastor must ask himself the "ease versus need" questions: Do I wait for an ideal setting? Do I seek an easy place? Or do I ask God to empower me to make this present assignment the opportunity I dreamed about?

The compelling issue is whether you want usefulness, ease, fruitfulness, opportunity or satisfaction. Sometimes opportunity and satisfaction fit together in an assignment. On the contrary, the most fruitful places may be demanding and difficult.

God may want you as a modern Moses in Memphis, Los Angeles, Shreveport, Lansing or Ord Bend. He might want to empower you to find holy ground in a messy, noisy place where anarchy and brokenness and dysfunction reign. Or His plan for your holy ground might be a delightful church like Paul enjoyed at Philippi. In any event, it is not essential that you be happy but that you matter, that you make a difference.

LESSONS FROM MOSES IN THE BADLANDS

Some modern ministry settings seem as barren as Moses' desert experience described in Exodus 3 where he cared for smelly sheep in the scorching sun. His situation probably was boring, and it is not too inspiring for us to consider, either.

Rethink the story. God impacted Moses at the burning bush in ways Moses could never forget. How could he? God came to Moses while he was performing ordinary work in a simple place, miles from fame of any kind. His setting was routine except for the burning bush, but that awareness of the presence of God made all the difference.

Miles from any action, God gave Moses a soul burden for his people. But Moses struggled to know what he could do about it. Like many present-day pastors, Moses was burdened for his people but didn't know how to help them.

Reading about Moses' encounter with the living God rekindles our motivation. Even a cursory reading of the story forces a reappraisal of our assignment and a reevaluation of our resources. What if Moses had been asked to figure out the logistics of moving all those people and their animals? From a human perspective, it would have been impossible. God intended to use Moses, and God had a plan.

How a pastor views himself, his competency, his spiritual maturity and God's direction also help determine outcomes in a specific setting.

For example, during a 20-year span, five pastors served a Colorado church. Ministers stayed for two to eight years. That congregation—

housed in the same building, same town and attended mostly by the same people or their kin—fluctuated from surviving to thriving. Although the fluctuation might be blamed on a variety of factors, the difference seemed to revolve around whether the pastor believed that the church and its congregation could make a difference.

To put the idea in loftier New Testament terms, God has built resurrection life into the fabric of every church. This supernatural force offers hope for revolutionizing a morally twisted society and for vitalizing a lethargic church again.

Pastors, like an army without bullets or bombs invading alien territory, hold the incredible energy of the gospel in their hands and in their hearts. Its power is amazing. It can penetrate the hardest soil. It's a supernatural power to cope with the minister's most demanding challenges. This makes spiritual triumphs possible in the toughest places.

Affirmations to the Modern Moses

Moses provides a life-changing model for contemporary pastors. His feeling of being sent by God kept him faithful for a lifetime. His willingness to be consumed by a mighty cause outweighed concerns about job satisfaction. For Moses, usefulness to God was more important than satisfaction, standing or security.

Moses' awareness of holy ground came as he opened the routines of his life to God. His curiosity caused him to say, "I will go over and see this strange sight—why the bush does not burn up" (Exod. 3:3).

No one knows how Moses would have reacted to all the risks facing modern clergy, such as membership migration, loss of absolutes and competition with technology, and to ever-changing paradigm shifts. We do know that complete dependance on God was the pattern of his life (see Exod. 3:11,12; 33:14-17). God's response was supernatural empowerment, as it always is (see Exod. 3:18-20).

Look Beyond Our Limitations

Looking beyond our limitations is a key point from Moses' life that motivates modern ministry. After hearing the *I AM* send him to blaze new trails of remarkable adventure and marvelous achievement, Moses could never view his situation the same old way. The same applies to us after we hear God's summons and recognize the potential He sees in our setting.

Even though Moses' problem of trying to lead stubborn people where they did not want to go may differ from ours, our need for God's empowerment is as intense as his was. God's assurance to Moses—"I am the God of your father, the God of Abraham, the God of Isaac and the God of Jacob....I will be with you" (Exod. 3:6,12)—is more than adequate to follow God's purposes for a lifetime. Being yoked with God in a holy cause makes every pastor a mighty vessel for righteousness in every setting.

Let's clarify the issues that all modern Moses-like pastors face. At this very moment, the future effectiveness of the gospel in thousands of settings is being determined by how pastors view their task and count their resources. Three pressing questions are before us:

1. Can we view our situation from God's perspective?
2. Can we believe every setting has more potential than anyone realizes?
3. Can we see ourselves as more than conquerors through the One who called and sent us?

God Seeks Cheerful Naturalized Citizens

When God sends them, modern Moseses must willingly go to tough places. Check two realities we seldom discuss:

1. There are not enough easy assignments to go around.
2. Most desirable places were difficult until a previous pastor loved the church into greatness. Face it—few Camelots exist in the ministry.

This means that ministers must sink their roots where the Father providentially places them. Jeremiah, the prophet, admonished the surviving elders who were exiled in Babylon: "Build houses and settle down; plant gardens and eat what they produce....Also, seek the peace and prosperity of the city to which I have carried you into exile. Pray to the Lord for it, because if it prospers, you too will prosper" (Jer. 29:5-7).

Pastors find themselves in situations they dislike, in towns they despise and working among people unlike any they have ever known. Endurance must be transformed into adventure. Resignation is better than rebellion, and a stiff upper lip is better than subtle resistance. It's

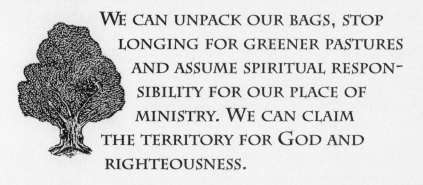

WE CAN UNPACK OUR BAGS, STOP LONGING FOR GREENER PASTURES AND ASSUME SPIRITUAL RESPON- SIBILITY FOR OUR PLACE OF MINISTRY. WE CAN CLAIM THE TERRITORY FOR GOD AND RIGHTEOUSNESS.

easy to choose tears, self-pity and complaints. But joy and fulfillment and unconditional involvement can be chosen. We can unpack our bags, stop longing for greener pastures and assume spiritual responsibility for our place of ministry. We can claim the territory for God and righteousness.

A pastor in Arizona wrote to me (Neil), explaining how he considers his present assignment as a long-term commitment. He purchased cemetery plots for himself and for his wife in the town where they were serving.

Pastors must commit to stay in an assignment until God gives them a genuine spiritual breakthrough or a clear-cut release. Many pastors need to become enthusiastic naturalized citizens of the place where they serve until they are used by God to establish a flourishing ministry.

God is pleased when a pastor welcomes a congregation into his heart and loves them as his extended family. He is pleased when a pastor learns to love an assignment as much as an ancestral home. He calls a pastor to be willing to live and to die for the congregation. Hundreds of churches have reason to think like a Methodist layman who wondered, "Why does the bishop keep sending us pastors who do not want to come here?" This needs to be changed.

Just as every pastor is strengthened and affirmed when laypeople love him, so every congregation thrives when the members know their pastor loves them. This two-way pattern is the amazing love relationship of the shepherd and the sheep that Jesus explained in John 10.

God Has Up-to-Date Plans

God's agenda is bigger than ours, and His plans are exceedingly in touch with contemporary needs. He is as fully acquainted with the future as with the past. He wants brokenness healed. He wants stony soils softened by selfless service. He wants secularists saved from themselves. He wants dysfunctional people and families made whole.

He also wants troublesome and immature church members served and nurtured because we are the only pastors they have. Although God's blueprint may seem too big or too complicated to us, He plans to accomplish His purposes through ordinary people like us.

In God's plan, much work needs to be accomplished outside the Church. Read the morning newspaper or listen to the evening news to be reminded of places where Christ must be taken. Think of yippies, immigrants, teens, single parents, homeless people, seniors, children, boomers and busters who have no experiential knowledge of Christ.

Consider violent city streets, dying rural towns, sophisticated centers of culture and sprawling suburbs. Arid spiritual wildernesses wait to be transformed into lush gardens where the gospel seed will bear abundant fruit and where Jesus is the Master Gardener. Could we pray to be inspired to live out new commitments that override all questions about hardship, inconvenience and frustration?

God Uses Unconditional Commitment

Words about unconditional commitment are difficult for us to hear and are even harder for us to live out in the details of ministry.

I (Neil) know a great pastor who during his pastoral prime in the early 1950s moved to a troubled church in western Kansas. For 15 years in Yakima, Washington, he had served a 350-member church with distinction. He had an impressive list of ministry achievements. He loved people and preached with a creative anointing. The church grew year after year in numbers and in spiritual vibrancy. He had no logical reason to move, but he did.

In the sunflower state assignment, everything went wrong from the start. Some members thought he was too progressive while others thought he was too old-fashioned. After a couple of years of misery, the decision group requested his resignation, and he submitted it. He had no place to go, however. He had little money.

The contrast between the loving congregation in Washington and his rejection in Kansas ate like a cancer at his sense of self-worth. He called his former district superintendent in the Northwest to discuss his dilemma. He was desperate and asked to be considered for any size church. The superintendent responded: "I would be glad to have you back in our area, but we have no openings. Sorry." The superintendent really meant that he had no openings that would fit the minister's capability and years of experience.

Throughout the night, the superintendent felt troubled as he pondered this great pastor's predicament. So he phoned early the next morning and said, "We have an opening in an isolated town. The church is so tiny I'm embarrassed to even suggest you go there. But I have an idea that will help you and will help this smaller church. Why don't you serve there for a few months until a stronger church opens. The smaller church will be flattered to have you even for a short time. In fact, you will be the most experienced pastor they have ever had."

My pastor friend accepted the challenge. He moved to that isolated town of 10,000 and to a church attended by fewer than 75 people. He told his friends the challenge was as exciting as his first pastorate years before. Opportunities to move to larger assignments soon beckoned. But to everyone's amazement, he stayed in the community for 10 years.

His commitment and competence made holy ground out of a tough place. Soon, the little church was the talk of the town, and it grew. New people began attending. The pastor started a daily 6:00 A.M. radio program that gave people a spiritual jump start as they went to their jobs or to work on their farms.

In a short time, everyone in the county knew him. He became chaplain of two service clubs. He was invited to speak during civic functions. He read books on writing and attended writing seminars; he wrote five books during the decade he served there. He also served as an inspirational model to younger pastors.

When asked about his tenure in such an ordinary place, he laughed and answered: "I found a secret here. People in this fine church were waiting for someone to love them, so I did. And they have loved me back."

My friend committed himself to the greatest thing in the entire world— to be used of God. One entry in his journal from those years follows: "As my contact with need increases, each completed project exposes me to many more waiting areas of service. Each task seems to open new opportunities of service and increases the circumference of my influence."

He demonstrated the old but ever new adventure of self-crucifixion to security, to place and to prominence.

God Nullifies Every Excuse

Overhearing conversations between God and Moses questions all our self-centered rationalizations. Listen again to lessons from Exodus 3 and 4.

Lesson 1: No need for self-pity or to complain, "Why me?"

God answers, "I will be with you and that is enough."

Lesson 2: No use to sniffle, "What if they do not believe me or listen to me and say, 'The Lord did not appear to you'?"

With unbelievable assurance God assures Moses, "I'll give you a miracle or two to inspire you and to capture their attention."

Lesson 3: No need to point out inadequacies or low self-esteem: "O Lord, I have never been eloquent, neither in the past nor since you have spoken to your servant. I am slow of speech and tongue."

God, weary of Moses' rationalizations, responds with a command and a promise, "Go. I will help you speak and will teach you what to say."

Lesson 4: No use to suggest that God send someone else: "O Lord, please send someone else to do it."

God answers with a promise: "I will give you someone to help you, and I will give both of you resources to speak and will teach you what to do."

Because the assets are significantly larger than the obstacles, let's refocus our vision. The rest of this decade and the new century promise to be a time of frightening resistance and of incredible productivity for the gospel. We will maximize the possibilities only if we approach our task with creative imagination, alert competence and unconditional dependence on God.

Most of all, the task before us demands an abiding assurance that God is with us. It calls for vigorous confidence that the gospel is the only answer to the moral mess that society faces. The time has come to make Christ-centered character, spiritual wholeness and Kingdom service attractive and fashionable again.

CONTEMPORARY CHALLENGE
YOUR PASTORATE IS HOLY GROUND

- Every congregation and community has untapped potential.
- Potential awareness starts with an encounter with God.
- Every church is an instrument for righteousness God wants to use.
- Every church can enjoy supernatural resurrection power.
- God nullifies every excuse we make.

Whatever our responsibilities, we are guest authorities, serving for a time, at the pleasure of our Lord, with persons and projects we do not own. —James D. Whitehead[4]

Notes

1. Bill Bright, editor, *The Greatest Lesson* (San Bernardino, CA: Here's Life Publishers, 1991), p. 173.
2. Eugene H. Peterson, *The Message* (Colorado Springs: NavPress, 1993), p. 221.

3.   William Willimon, "Pumping Truth to a Disinclined World," *Leadership*,
     Vol. XI, No. 2 (Spring 1990), p. 136.
4.   James D. Whitehead, *The Promise of Partnership* (San Francisco:
     HarperSanFrancisco, 1991), p. 112.

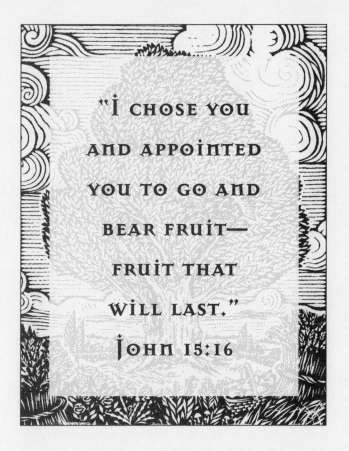

"I CHOSE YOU
AND APPOINTED
YOU TO GO AND
BEAR FRUIT—
FRUIT THAT
WILL LAST."
JOHN 15:16

2

PARTNERSHIP WITH THE MASTER GARDENER

God—living Lord, I rejoice in our relationship where You are senior partner in my ministry. Help me see Your plans for this place. Help me follow Your will to the last detail. Sharpen my awareness of the potential around me. Save me from self-sufficiency. And help me make this field produce lasting fruit.
Amen.

THE MASTER GARDENER HAS A PLAN FOR YOUR SETTING

Jesus sets the agenda for holy ground ministry with His directive to go everywhere and to win everyone. The adventure in this assignment is brought into crystal-clear focus when we examine the parable of the sower in the light of Jesus' commission to win everyone everywhere.

You Are a Farm and a Field

A few years ago, Bob Benson, an author and speaker, remarked during a Kentucky retreat that "we should be glad Jesus thinks of us as a farm as well as a field." His point, of course, was that few people, including pastors, hear the Word of God without the message being hindered in some way.

Accurate listening can be thwarted by rootless enthusiasms, by frightening persecutions, by discouraging troubles, by worries of life, by deceitfulness of wealth or, for pastors, by the deceitfulness of not having wealth.

Ministers as well as believers can be like the farm in our Lord's parable of the sower (see Luke 8:4-8). We are made up of fields, some productive and others barren, rocky, packed down or overrun with thorns. I hope it does not push the meaning of the parable too far to suggest at least that some ministry crises might appear in a field that has become overly focused on troubles, persecutions, cares of this life and cunning of riches.

During his lifetime, every pastor knows the feeling that one or two fields are flourishing for the cause of Christ while other fields are weedy, stony and unproductive.

You Hold Incredible Seed in Your Hand

The law of harvest promises that you will reap the kind of fruit you plant. All of us need new confidence in what the gospel seed can reproduce— righteousness produces righteousness just as surely as onions produce onions. Too often we mistakenly expect to reap righteousness by sowing something else.

Continue sowing the good news of the gospel. Even though the weather may turn bad some years, the harvest will produce redeemed people and renewed churches.

Cultivate Every Field

Even the richest soil has to be tilled faithfully and frequently. The same is true of the Church.

In the agricultural world, good soil only produces a crop of grass and weeds until the ground is plowed, planted, watered, cultivated and harvested.

For the minister, this means that many apparently unattractive and overgrown church settings are rich in opportunity beyond our wildest imagination. In many places, a bumper crop awaits the pastor who cultivates the land and plants the gospel seed.

Farming Is Hard Work
The parable of the sower teaches that no harvest can be expected with-

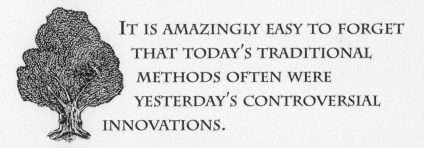

IT IS AMAZINGLY EASY TO FORGET THAT TODAY'S TRADITIONAL METHODS OFTEN WERE YESTERDAY'S CONTROVERSIAL INNOVATIONS.

out effort. Ministry is hard work. It is not without joy or adventure or effectiveness, but it is tough and demanding.

A young pastor in his first assignment in a small growing southern Michigan church said, "I never enjoyed hard work so much as I do in this ministry. I start early in the morning and work all day. But it is fun taking the message of Christ into people's lives in such a variety of ways."

Faithful farming is a continuous requirement throughout the entire growing season. All this compels a pastor to keep on planting, weeding, cultivating, feeding the soil and bringing in the harvest before bad weather strikes.

Results May Seem Slow
Acorns grow much slower than dandelions. Patient waiting can be one of the most frustrating experiences of ministry, but gospel planting and harvesting often require abundant persistence. Consider the possibilities, however.

Everyone knows at least one believer who delayed responding to the gospel for years. In spite of no visible results, someone kept sowing and cultivating until the seed finally germinated into a harvest of righteousness. That's the way it frequently happens. Keep working the fields and keep planting the seed. A harvest is on the horizon.

It's Time to Break New Ground

A cynic's comment is too close to truth for comfort: "Futurists say knowledge changes every five years, but the Church takes 40 years to consider changing her Sunday morning schedule and then votes against it." Although the skeptic may have overstated the case, the Church has a well-earned reputation for resisting change or for seeing no need for it.

Throughout Church history, lay members have been notorious for believing modification of methods were a compromise of truth. Technique and truth, in many minds, are identical twins. It is amazingly easy to forget that today's traditional methods often were yesterday's controversial innovations.

Sadly, many golden opportunities are missed when a church resists change, even under the guise of lofty cautiousness. We can become so heavenly minded we no longer are of earthly good. As one pastor observed: "Holding the line often means missing the boat." Then new challenges, new populations and new centers of society are left untouched by the gospel.

In our confusion over rapid change in our culture, it is easy to overlook the fact that biblical accounts of the Early Church are packed with innovative strategies that took the Christian message to unevangelized places, nationalities, races and cultures. That is our task, too!

WAYS TO CULTIVATE HOLY GROUND

New settings and rapid societal changes require fresh ways to communicate changeless truth. Without creativity, imagination and a commitment to the future, we will miss magnificent opportunities to impact the new century with the gospel.

How can we increase productivity in our present pastorates? How can we rekindle a sense of Christ's mission for His Church and not merely support the institution?

Keep the Door Open to Innovation
Because change is ever present, why not stop resisting it and start using it? Observe and use trends in society to shape new ways to minister. Watch for changes in the way people view life and how they respond to the work of the church.

Take risks. Remember, given enough time, the status quo often collapses under its own weight. Concentrate on keeping your message Christ-centered and your mission rooted in New Testament teaching, and then dare to change your methods.

Risky Christianity, in many ways, is a willingness to take a chance on death so that the cause may live and flourish.

Admit Everything Is Not Okay
To acknowledge frailties in the Church and failures in the ministry is a giant step toward renewal. Psychologists speak of a "professional denial reflex" in many occupations that occurs when rapid change and threats of job loss are present. This may be why some religious leaders are unwilling to admit that anything in the Church needs to be fixed.

I heard a recognized clergy leader tell ministerial students a few days ago during chapel that "the Church is doing a better job of fulfilling her mission now than at any time in church history." A student asked a friend seated next to him, "I wonder if the speaker really believes that? If everything is right, why are so many giving up on the Church?"

Let's admit that the Church is not what it should be. It is not what it can be. Deep in our hearts, we all know the Church needs to be renewed and refocused. There is a growing feeling among pastors that something has to be done about it.

Neither does it help to gloss over the Church's weakness by recounting the opportunities available to her. We often hear that these are days of golden opportunity for the Church, and so they are.

An enormous difference exists, however, between opportunity and achievement. Although this is a day of gigantic potential, if opportunity is measured by human need, it is not a day of achievement when so much church growth has become a mere shifting of members between congregations and denominations. In a recent survey, George Barna, a church researcher, underscored that as much as 80 percent of all church growth is the result of "the saints" moving from one church to the next.

Winston Churchill is quoted as saying that challenges are keys to self-renewal. If he is right, the Church is presented with the potential of an awesome awakening.

Restore the Supernatural

In pastoral routines, it is easy to forget that ministry at its core has a supernatural linkage with the resources of God. Although most pastors can preach, counsel, visit, comfort, raise funds or lead without divine enablement, everyone does it better with God's help.

All efforts will be more lasting when divine anointing, presence, unction and guidance are restored to the daily activities of ministry. In the process, many of the reasons pastors quit or burn out turn out to be somewhat superficial when compared with the supernatural.

God never intended a pastor's work to be mere human effort. A pastor wrote to H. B. at Focus on the Family, revealing that his frustrations with his decision-making group dropped to zero when he invited Christ to attend every meeting with him. "I should have known all along that God is as interested in those meetings as I am," he rejoiced. "Now each meeting has become a ministry occasion where lay leaders openly seek to serve each other. It is a wonderful change!"

Commit to a Moral Awakening

Due to the mind-boggling moral chaos and ethical irrationality in our society, a reawakening is an absolute necessity. Something more than syrupy spiritual sentimentality is needed. Society is drowning in a moral cesspool.

One commentator called our situation "a civil war for the soul of the nation."[1] Another media giant wishes for "a sudden epidemic of common sense."[2] Violence, despair and sin infect modern life like lethal poisons.

A moral reawakening of the magnitude we need depends on thousands of smaller revolutionary moral changes in every hamlet, crossroad, small town, suburb, city, county and state. It won't come from imposing halls of government but from simple houses of worship. It won't come from centers of learning at the universities but from resurrection power proclaimed from hundreds of pulpits. It won't come from TV talk shows but from intercessory prayer meetings.

This kind of reawakening will require heroic leaders who speak against sinful practices. It will take pastors who challenge church members and communities to moral rightness and adventuresome faith, even at the risk of being labeled as far-right bigots or leftover Puritan fogies.

Our present situation could provide an astonishing window of opportunity for the cause of Christ if William Bennett, education director and later drug czar during the Bush administration, is right: "People are recognizing that religion is a domain we ignore at our peril." He adds a sober warning: "But too many people still treat religion as if it's simply a small part of life, as if it is a little compartment and a little category, like aerobics and aesthetics and athletics."[3]

Assess your assets again. These could be the best of times for the Christian message if we know what to do with them. That means that every gospel assignment is holy ground, and serious ministers of the gospel must commit to a moral awakening in their sphere of influence, no matter how large or small they believe their influence is.

Abolish Meaninglessness
People are bone weary of meaninglessness. George Barna summarizes the current dilemma:

> Consider all the crises, failures and disappointments wrought by the warped or unrealistic standards and expectations embodied by the '80s. Materialism was tried but found lacking. Religion was expected to clarify our purpose and values, but it generally did not. Sexual experimentation and promiscuity proved incapable of satiating our sexual and emotional appetites. The best efforts of government failed to solve our emotional, spiritual and physical problems. The continual

restructuring of the traditional family has caused much con-
sternation but produced little productive response.[4]

People are cruelly disillusioned by the fact that they invested monumental energy and unbelievable commitment to reach the top only to
find that it does not satisfy or that someone else got there first. They
learn that money does not buy meaning and security does not produce
satisfaction.

The Creator implanted a hunger in the human psyche to make sense
of life. Everyone wants to make his life count. Everyone needs to make a
life as well as a living.

Two *New York Times* reports underscore this increasing search for meaning.

Dr. Charles W. Hickman, director of projects and services for the
American Assembly of Collegiate Schools, while discussing declining
interest of students entering graduate programs in business remarked,
"Today's students view contributing to society and improving lives of
other people as more important than financial rewards."[5]

On the same day, President Bill Clinton announced that "unless we
reach deep into the values, the spirit, the soul, the truth of human nature,
none of the other things we seek to do will ever take us to where we want
to go."[6]

This sounds like a golden opportunity to teach and demonstrate the
authentic meaning and the full joy that Christ brings into human life.
Masses of people will be magnetically attracted to the Church when she
recaptures more meaning for what she does. The Church must speak
much more precisely about her magnificent mission to transform the
world and to give meaning to individuals.

For individuals, the Christ-way is the best possible life. This way of
living provides ultimate payoffs on the *last* day when we stand before
God. Before then, we enjoy an amazing quality of life as we become
more like Christ. This kind of life is fulfilling and satisfying. Such a focus
in ministry encourages people to seek a growing relationship with Christ.

Such an emphasis on meaning helps a pastor lead people to the full
satisfaction that spirituality and service provide. Everyone wants to make

his life count, and that is the central benefit of the Christian life.

"Repot" Your Ministry

"Repot" means to transplant a plant to a bigger pot so it is not root bound and the roots have room to grow. This term, when used in relation to vocational issues, comes from John R. O'Neil, author and statesman, who describes "repotting" as a purposeful choice to enjoy the excitement of

> THE WORLD NEEDS SPOKESPERSONS TO TAKE THE GOOD NEWS OF CHRIST TO EVERY SOCIAL AND ECONOMIC CLASS. ALL PEOPLE NEED THE GOSPEL, AND WE MUST TAKE IT TO THEM IN WORDS THEY UNDERSTAND WITHOUT ANY FEELINGS OF PERSONAL INTIMIDATION ON OUR PART.

doing what you are doing better or trying something new or expanding your interests to new fields.[7]

Repotting possibilities are nearly limitless for a pastor. You can improve your preaching or counseling skills. You can refresh your Greek. You can take a college course in human relationships or in creative writing. You can plan a day of spiritual retreat every month. You can give yourself growing room in your present setting so you perform your work with more passion and understanding.

Try "repotting" your ministry. Allow the mental picture of a plant being given room to expand its root system to impact your ministry and to reshape your personal and professional growth.

Resist Cultural Intimidation

Secularism, sophistication and security are dead-end streets, even though much of society acts as if all three are worthy life goals. As a result, pastors sometimes feel browbeaten by society's values. As Christ's followers, we must recognize that those who are locked into such secular value systems need the good news of the gospel as much as anyone.

On Mars Hill, Paul provides a pattern for such a ministry. In addressing Epicurean and Stoic philosophers, Paul proclaimed at the Areopagus:

> "From one man he [God] made every nation of men, that they should inhabit the whole earth; and he determined the times set for them and the exact places where they should live. God did this so that men would seek him and perhaps reach out for him and find him, though he is not far from each one of us. 'For in him we live and move and have our being'" (Acts 17:26-28).

Note that Paul used verbal symbols his hearers easily understood; he spoke the language of their social standing and class like a missionary using a native language dialect. In the process, he did not fear cultural opposition, nor did he water down the gospel to please his hearers.

Even as missionaries are needed to take the ministry into alien nations and cultures, so the world needs spokespersons to take the good news of Christ to every social and economic class. All people need the gospel, and we must take it to them in words they understand without any feelings of personal intimidation on our part.

More and more potential settings for the gospel message are being misshaped by secularism, by sophistication and by security. Many people will not understand the basic vocabulary of faith, nor do they have a Christian memory. But they need us, and we must go to them, using Paul's strategies.

- Speak so secularists understand.
- Take the gospel to every strata of society.
- Use transferable concepts.
- Start with familiar ideas.
- Emphasize resurrection power.
- Conquer your fear of new cultural environments.
- Believe God wants to transform everyone.

Create a Future for Ministry

Demographics, social trends, expert research and investigative analysis are useful for helping us understand our world and our opportunities. But there is more.

Hal Leavitt, speaking as a professor at Stanford's Graduate School of Business, once remarked, "There is more emphasis on predicting the future than on making the future."[8] His synopsis applies to the Church because some of her most significant accomplishments have sometimes surprised her leaders. One anonymous Christian leader explained, "The Holy Spirit plays tricks on the Church by doing new things in nearly every generation."

To predict the future is passive, but to shape the future is active. Predicting the future means we attempt to explain what appears to be inevitable. But shaping and fashioning the future starts by asking what God wants the gospel to accomplish in the new generation and then working to make it happen.

George Gallup has a prescription to shape the process. He advises:

- LISTEN to the remarkable spiritual experiences of people and help them understand and build upon these experiences.
- TEACH people how to develop their faith, pray more effectively, bring the Bible into their daily lives and become better trained in leadership skills.
- ENCOURAGE small-group fellowships, which serve as a means for people to enter the faith community as well as a way to support current members.
- INSPIRE people to reach out to others in appropriate and loving ways.
- TARGET key groups for spiritual nourishment and religious instruction: people in business, the professions and other fields who constantly make ethical judgments; students, who receive an incomplete and distorted education if the vital role of religion is ignored; and people in the media, who often are ignorant about religion.[9]

Future victories in spiritually depressing times will be accomplished by those who light bright lights in dark places. Russell Chandler, retired religious reporter for the *Los Angeles Times*, tells us why we must prepare for the future: "We need anticipation and understanding, yes. Even more, we need help to harness the forces of change for our personal and collective journey."[10]

Who would be willing to settle for what appears inevitable when he could shape the Church into what Christ wants it to be?

Produce Magnificent Fruit

Years ago, a couple who were pastors to a midsize church in Idaho, took turns preaching on alternate Sundays. In addition to being a wife and mother, the woman was an interesting biblical expositor to whom the people enjoyed listening. The man, though a highly appreciated pastor, was introspective, shy, sometimes melancholy and not a gifted speaker.

When it was his Sunday to preach, he usually awoke with discouraging self-doubts and discussed them openly. On those Sundays, it was his custom during breakfast to express his apprehension and to ask his wife and children to pray for him. He freely admitted he was unsure of his message, questioned his ability to speak and wondered how close he really was to Christ. It was a bad scene for everyone in the family and a terribly discouraging way to begin Sunday.

"God, help Edward," his wife would pray as she helped the children prepare for church. "You know he can do it. And You will help him. He has served You faithfully all week, and You will help him now."

This pastor's wife has an important message for contemporary clergy members. Even in confusing times, we can accomplish competent ministry because of God's enablement. Joshua 1:9 promises: "Be strong and courageous. Do not be terrified; do not be discouraged, for the Lord your God will be with you wherever you go."

Take strength for every part of your ministry as you consider God's remarkable record of helping ordinary people in difficult circumstances. Consider their victories as promises for your own victory:

- Daniel slept peaceably in a den of lions.
- Joseph resisted a seductive woman.
- David overpowered a giant.
- Elijah defied a heathen cult.
- John the Baptist redirected his prominence to Jesus.
- Paul sang stress away at midnight in jail.
- Jesus modeled God's love on the middle cross.

This list contains enough encouragement to reenergize your ministry even in the most demanding setting. Join hands and hearts with hundreds of self-renewing pastors who are committed to taking the gospel to the cutting edge of modern life.

Participants will experience a magnificent soul-stretching sense of God's nearness in the middle of a ministry filled to the brim with incredible demands, challenging possibilities and remarkable achievements.

A Mentor's Letter
Concerning Holy Ground

Recently, I wrote to a young pastor who was feeling shell shocked at the first anniversary of his first pastorate. Nothing was the way he believed it should be. He wanted to quit, wanted to go back to school to learn how to train pastors. Here's part of my letter to him:

"Finding holy ground for ministry is not to go, but to stay. It is not to look for something else, but to see what you already have. It is not to hunger for a new love, but to court an old one. It is not to long for ease, but to risk everything to cultivate your stony field until it produces an abundant crop.

"It is not to quit too soon, but to persevere until you would not consider leaving. It is not to give your difficulties so much attention, but to invest more energy in nourishing the center of your faith so God can use you for a radical renewal in the congregation you serve. Yours for faithfulness and effectiveness, too."

CONTEMPORARY CHALLENGE
A PROLIFIC PARTNERSHIP WITH GOD

- God's nearness makes ministry an adventure regardless of location.
- People in your setting have incredible spiritual needs.
- Your outlook limits or liberates ministry.
- The gospel seed penetrates the hardest soil.
- God has up-to-date plans for every setting.
- Everyone—pastor, parishioners and the world—need a miracle.

No good work is done anywhere without aid from the Father of Lights. —C. S. Lewis[11]

Notes
1. Cal Thomas, *Denver Post*, Dec. 25, 1993, 4G.
2. Bill Moyers, *USA Weekend*, Dec. 26, 1993, 4A.
3. William Bennett, *Colorado Springs Gazette Telegraph*, Oct. 6, 1993, 13A.
4. George Barna, *The Barna Report 1993-94, Absolute Confusion* (Ventura, CA: Regal Books, 1993), p. 20.
5. Charles W. Hickman, *New York Times*, Nov. 14, 1993, 18Y.

6. William Clinton, *New York Times*, Nov. 14, 1993, 19Y.
7. John R. O'Neil, *The Paradox of Success* (New York: Putnam & Sons, 1993), p. 163.
8. Danny Cox and John Hoover, *Leadership When the Heat's On* (New York: McGraw-Hill, 1992), p. 195.
9. George Gallup, as quoted in *Racing Toward 2001* by Russell Chandler (San Francisco: HarperSanFrancisco, 1992), p. 313.
10. Russell Chandler, *Racing Toward 2001*, p. 313.
11. Wayne Martindale and Jerry Root, *The Quotable Lewis* (Wheaton, IL: Tyndale House Publishers, 1989), p. 270.

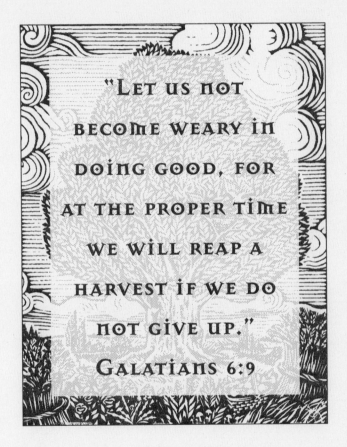

"LET US NOT BECOME WEARY IN DOING GOOD, FOR AT THE PROPER TIME WE WILL REAP A HARVEST IF WE DO NOT GIVE UP."

GALATIANS 6:9

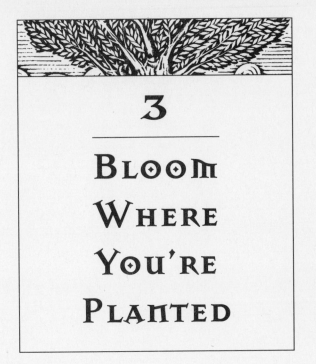

3

BLOOM
WHERE
YOU'RE
PLANTED

Master Gardener of my soul and ministry,
Open my eyes to opportunities in my assignment.
Open my affections to the unique beauty and possibilities in this
place. And strengthen my skills to be Your junior gardener to
plant, water, cultivate, weed, prune and harvest in this place.
Amen.

MAXIMIZE OPPORTUNITIES

"Bloom Busters helped me grow these flowers, the greatest gardening success I've ever had," the shopkeeper in Red Stone, Colorado, said in response to my comments about her flowers. She had the most extraordinary red geraniums I (Neil) had ever seen. Garden catalog illustrations seem inferior by comparison.

At the first sign of spring, you can be sure I started shopping for Bloom Busters. I found several plant foods with similar names, but I never located Bloom Busters.

The shopkeeper might have misspoken. Maybe I misunderstood, or perhaps I did not shop in the right stores. But if Bloom Busters does not exist, some entrepreneur should market a plant food by that name.

That name started me thinking about frontline pastors I know. They do everything they can to be a vessel for God in a hurting world. They work and pray and struggle. Yet, in spite of their sacrificial commitments and demanding schedules, their churches often grow only slightly or shrink a little every year. Like working in a wilting garden in a scorching August sun, their sizable efforts never break growth barriers. Nothing unusual happens in their congregations.

They feel like the tired old preacher who said, "My necessities ate up my possibilities." They starve for the reality they lost when ministry was allowed to become secularized, professionalized, miniaturized and marginalized. They hunger for a new grip on ministry.

They seek a fresh anointing and a new perspective. They want something to happen inside them similar to the 40-year-old pastor who reported after serving his rural Georgia church for 10 years, "When I allowed myself to be fascinated by opportunities and by the grace of God, I started blooming in ways I never experienced before."

New ministry blooming in familiar places requires that we take a discriminating look at existing ministry activities even as we carefully scrutinize our opportunities. Most settings have extraordinary possibilities that no one may envision on the surface. For example, outreach makes ministry grow faster than administrative activities do, and marriage workshops usually are more effective than divorce restoration counseling.

A beginning New England pastor wrote to me, saying, "I don't have time for outreach because I am too busy studying for next Sunday's sermon, stomping out brush fires and trying to meet the unrealistic demands of people in the church."

Could it be that more emphasis on outreach would change the focus of his ministry and would challenge the perceptions of the members of his small church? Making such a shift would be tough, but it is the only way new opportunities for his church will be set in motion.

Larger Blooms and Lasting Fruit

One reality is obvious: God wants every ministry to bloom, to bear magnificent fruit and to have strong roots. He wants His people fed and loved in every place. He does not, however, expect each pastor to look alike, to grow at the same rate or to have the same impact. That is why He planted you where you are.

Several key challenges must be faced if ministry in a specific place is to be renewed, reenergized or even revolutionized. Try scoring yourself on this checklist:

- Am I willing and able to revitalize and to restate my ministry so it attracts contemporary people?
- Can I take the life-changing force of the gospel to the cutting edges of life where the substitutes for faith have proven trivial and futile?
- Can I help secular people see the gospel as an appealing alternative to the security, sex, fame and power they chase?
- Can one pastor change the world?
- Can my ministry thrive in a tough place where effective ministry has never occurred?
- What did God have in mind for me to accomplish in this place when He called me here?

Everyone knows that flourishing gardens need quality seed, cultivating, watering, weeding and meticulous attention to soil conditions and temperature. But my Red Stone gardener friend multiplied her success and satisfaction when she added generous amounts of tender loving care and nourishing plant food.

Ministry is like that—tender loving care and bloom busters must be added to grow spiritually vibrant congregations. After years of developing believers in my own churches and observing hundreds of pastors at work, I believe these bloom busters will make ministry flourish and will enable pastors to bloom where God has planted them.

Try them for yourself. I guarantee you that the people you serve will remember more about the person you are than about the words you say.

MEASURE POTENTIAL GOD'S WAY

I loved the way one church described itself in an advertisement seeking a new pastor:

> A DIAMOND IN THE ROUGH is searching for a master stonecutter to unleash the potential that lies beneath its surface. This GEM TO BE can be found in a suburban neighborhood in South-Central Pennsylvania....If you have a steady hand, keen eye, and are willing to "strike the blow" to produce dazzling results, write to....[1]

Maybe every church is a diamond in the rough, waiting for a master stonecutter to strike the blow to unleash its potential.

View Your Church as a Living Cell

Take another careful look at your diamond in the rough.

In *Diary of a Country Priest*, Georges Bernanos writes tenderly about his congregation: "This morning I prayed hard for my parish, my poor parish, my first and perhaps my last, since I ask no better than to die here. My parish! The words can't even be spoken without a kind of soaring love....I know that my parish is a reality; it is not a mere administrative segment, but a living cell of the everlasting Church."[2]

It is nearly impossible for a pastor to see his church as a living cell of the everlasting Church when he is bogged down with the confusing expectations of dear old Sister Smith or while he is dealing with the sad sorrow of a dying teenager. This is probably the reason pastors usually see more problems than possibilities in the place where the Father has planted them. The inability to see the forest because we are in the midst of the trees certainly applies.

Can you see it clearly and believe it thoroughly? Your church is a living cell of the everlasting Church.

Play Prospective Pastor

To reevaluate your opportunities, try playing prospective pastor for a full day once or twice each year. Drive or walk through your surroundings as if you were seeing the setting for the first time. Refocus on the potential you saw when you first visited this place.

Dare to dream your original dream again. See your congregation as live, flesh-and-blood people—some noble and some neurotic, some saintly and some sinful, some great and some not so great. The routines you feel and experience day after day or year after year may become brand new. Remember, God intends for ministry to thrive everywhere people reside.

Recently, a bored young pastor phoned to ask, "What comes next after pastoring?" He continued, "I've been thinking about trying teaching or law or social work." What comes next? His question implies he does not measure potential in his church the way God does.

All things considered, who could be satisfied with the narrower spiritual opportunities other occupations offer when a person could be a pastor? The possibilities are enormous and eternal. To see them clearly, every parish minister needs to pray often, "God, show me what You want done in this part of Your harvest."

Opportunity blindness always worsens when a pastor considers each assignment as a stepping stone to something better. Such a stance forces him to consider every pastorate as semitemporary, and in some unexplainable, self-fulfilling way, his thinking causes the assignment to actually become restrictive and suffocating and enslaving. Without his realizing it, opportunities he hopes to find in another place often already exist where he resides.

Francis Bacon's advice helps us bloom: "A wise man makes more opportunities than he finds."[3] I would imagine that any long-term pastor has considered moving to another place only to be reminded by the Lord, "I have not released you; I need you here; your work is not finished."

Marking Time Costs Too Much

The human cost of marking time, while waiting for something better, can be frighteningly high. Those we could have won for Christ continue in their sinful alienation. Broken homes we could have mended go to the divorce courts. Innocent children we could have introduced to the Savior move on to adulthood without hearing the name of Jesus. Church members atrophy. Our passion for service shrivels.

Multiply these losses across a few thousand congregations and it adds up to alarming spiritual barrenness for a country and a culture. As we approach the twenty-first century, the issue of apathy may be our number one problem. Possibilities are clouded when a pastor feels overwhelmed by the massive and compelling spiritual needs he sees around him everywhere. As a result, sin and secularism are devastatingly oppressive to him.

But consider the presuppositions of ministry again. Doesn't a call to ministry mean that God may send a pastor to wretched situations He wants to redeem and to people He wants to save? Doesn't ministry mean that God sends us, inadequate though we are, next door to hell to make the setting more like heaven? He has to have *someone* there as His agent of reconciliation.

A pastor yearning for an easy assignment is as strange as a missionary wanting to go to an overevangelized nation instead of a place where people have never heard about Christ.

Consider Two Perspectives from Jesus

Jesus viewed potential from two perspectives: while using a towel to wash dirty feet, and from the cross.

God usually assigns us to a place where we are most needed, even when we long for an easier place. God may need us in a tough place where the salary is low and the housing is limited. Perhaps He will assign us to places of urban decay, social violence or moral desperation. Maybe He will send us to congregations splintered by broken relationships. He might want us to serve brutal, greedy, exploitative people because we are their only hope.

Perhaps God intends for us to feed faith and love to people in places where they have given up and who may also be suspicious and hostile. Let's face it, pastors throughout the long, stirring march of Christian history have often bloomed best in moral barnyards.

When a pastor begins to evaluate potential from Jesus' perspective, every congregation possesses extraordinary possibilities. Every church and community then seems ready for a spiritual awakening. Of course, incredibly difficult assignments force a pastor to absolute dependence on God. Why be terrified or intimidated? We are linked in strength-giving partnership with omnipotence.

Create an Ideal Assignment

Maybe every minister dreams of a perfect pastorate—whatever that is. Many expect to be surprised by some ministerial fantasy around the next bend. Others hope their ideal will show up before Christmas.

Some people spend their entire ministry in search of a model congre-

> AN ABSOLUTELY INDISPENSABLE
> FACTOR IN SUSTAINING A
> HEALTHY MINISTRY IS THE
> WILLINGNESS FOR A PASTOR TO
> VIEW HIS SETTING FROM GOD'S
> PERSPECTIVE.

gation made up of hundreds of good-natured people in a moderate climate, in an ideal town, with high pay. Still others fret for years, coveting a task God never grants them. For many, it's wanting what the other guy has without considering the problems that go with it.

Apparently the pastors who long for greener pastures have never considered the reality that every good place requires someone to transform a tough assignment into a special, desirable church by blooming there. Such an idealized assignment may be similar to beauty in the eye of the beholder.

Ideal for someone will be a country congregation or a city storefront, a church planted in a new development or a 100-year-old congregation, or maybe a home Bible study group or a congregation of 500 or 5,000. The secret is to make your assignment ideal by blooming where God plants you.

Expanding our views of potential even more, a young pastor suggests wisdom beyond his years, "I do not think a minister should move until he has experienced a spiritual breakthrough where he is."

Careful, there is a surprising bear trap in his concept. He continues, "Who would ever want to leave a place while an authentic spiritual breakthrough is taking place?" This view helps us see incredible possibilities in every setting and undermines the human frustration and financial costs of moving to another church. An absolutely indispensable factor in sustaining a healthy ministry is the willingness to view one's setting from God's perspective.

A church leader in Canada suggests: "Every church has a right to have a pastor who believes something spiritually significant will happen in that place under his leadership. If a pastor does not believe in the possibilities of his assignment, he should seek God until he sees potentiality." More than mere strategy, this is the pastoral leadership tree trunk out of which branches of effective ministry grow.

God counts on you to achieve a miraculous ministry in the place where He has planted you. He has no one else to fill your place. Growing a magnificent ministry in any location can be started or renewed by finding a need that breaks your heart and then breaking your back to meet that need.

FIND FULFILLMENT WHERE YOU ARE

A yearning to be whole, to make his life count and to make a difference in the world are what make a potential pastor open to God's call into ministry. A nagging quest for meaning is a universal human hunger. Most of the world continues looking for the prize in the wrong places. But ministry majors on meaning.

A pastor on Florida's Gold Coast was called to a 100-member church made up of mostly elderly people. He followed a pastor who had served this congregation for more than 20 years. He had been there so long that few people in the congregation could remember the former pastor.

To complicate matters, many members of the congregation lived across the street from the church in a Social Security supplement high-rise building. As a result, the new pastor faced unusually heavy demands for pastoral care. Some of his minister friends warned him that the situation was futile, but he saw beyond the limitations.

In eight years, the new pastor started Bible studies in the high-rise facility, recruited immigrants from Haiti, Cuba, Mexico and Finland to start six language churches, began a youth ministry, purchased five near-by houses for sanctuary expansion and offered genuine friendship to the former pastor who lived nearby.

The new minister saw beyond age and color and language and limitation. After he had been there for several years, one of his friends who had advised him not to accept the pastorate offered this compliment: "You took lemons and made lemonade."

During an interview for a pastor's magazine in which he was asked about finding ministry fulfillment in tough assignments, this minister responded: "Complain about difficulties? Emphasize hardships? Bellyache about inconvenience? Many do and so could I. But what's the point? There's so much more to ministry. I choose to hope, explore, cherish, contribute and live. I enjoy seeing how much fun I can have in the ministry."

This minister's ability to find meaning, fulfillment and satisfaction was a natural result of a long succession of doing the right things for the right reasons across years of cheerful, Christ-centered service.

His formula for fulfillment: Expect every assignment to enrich your life and it will not disappoint you. The serendipity of selfless service is abiding satisfaction. Loving gives us love. Serving supplies satisfaction. Giving one's self away enriches us.

How to Increase Fulfillment

To increase satisfaction, rekindle your original motivations for ministry. Rejoice in your achievements. Celebrate your victories as God-given enablements that flow into the nooks and cubbyholes of your ministry.

Tame your workaholic tendencies so you can find time to grow a great soul. Read old and new books about ministry to establish a benchmark for your pastoral service. Find successful models to emulate. Doing these ecclesiastical calisthenics on a regular basis prevents spiritual stagnation and professional passivity and superficial success.

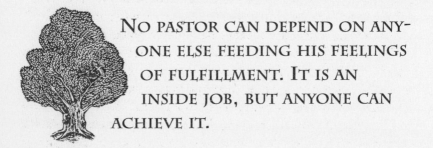

NO PASTOR CAN DEPEND ON ANY-ONE ELSE FEEDING HIS FEELINGS OF FULFILLMENT. IT IS AN INSIDE JOB, BUT ANYONE CAN ACHIEVE IT.

Let's admit that every pastor stands at the center of what makes ministry meaningful for him. The springs of fulfillment are internal and personal. The whole thing starts with that first stirring in your soul about ministry; no one else heard the dialogue and debate between you and God. Because God called you, it means you measure fulfillment differently from people in other occupations or other pastors. It means you are most fulfilled when God is most pleased with your ministry.

Fulfillment Is an Inside Job

Unless ministers find a high level of meaning in their work, they almost never significantly impact a congregation or a community. Take an example from army history: A subordinate on General George C. Marshall's staff during World War II reported that several officers were having low morale problems.

General Marshall retorted, "Officers don't have morale problems. Officers cure morale problems in themselves and others. No one looks after my morale."[4] He is probably right about military personnel, and he certainly says a lot to ministers. No pastor can depend on anyone else feeding his feelings of fulfillment. It is an inside job, but anyone can achieve it.

A pastor in a mid-Atlantic state, let's call him Tom, has served a series of congregations for 31 years. He is confused about when to expect his satisfactions. To a trusted friend, he spoke sadly.

"All my life, I followed scripts suggested by my parents, wife, church members and even my bishop. And when their scripts conflicted, I just tried harder. But I haven't experienced much fulfillment. I've done my duty, but it hasn't been too much fun. My life is melancholy and drab."

Now, at age 55, Tom keeps waiting for someone to give him his fulfillment, but he fears it will never come. And he's probably right.

How tragic! Tom should have awakened years ago to the fact that no outside circumstance or person provides meaning for a pastor. Fate does not assign anyone the task of making ministry meaningful for us.

Genuine fulfillment is rooted in knowing what ministry is and in doing it energetically and creatively. Better than anyone else, you know when your ministry is vibrant and satisfying. You know what pleases God. This is what matters most in measuring meaning in ministry.

Fulfillment Is an Intentional Choice

Unfortunately, a pastor never gains an ounce of fulfillment by saying, "I know I should build a satisfying ministry, but I don't get the breaks or have the luck or possess natural abilities." Far better to realize that every minister can have more meaning if and when he wants it.

Admittedly, finding fulfillment takes more work in some places than in others. But take heart! Pastor Ron Mehl of the Beaverton (Oregon) Foursquare Church explains the fountainhead of fulfillment, "God sees the fine, strong character qualities we will develop in the future while we see ourselves muddling through perplexity and setbacks and sudden reversals."[5] Many gospel harvest hands believe hardships produce the sweetest satisfactions.

One writer suggests that discovering fulfillment is like experiencing a hot stove. After touching a blistering flame, one can draw back forever and announce, "I will never touch a stove again."

A different reaction is more desirable. One can turn down the heat, follow the instruction book, have the stove repaired and become a gourmet cook. Then the cook has the satisfaction of serving a superb meal and many are well fed. In a similar way, pastors can either quit or find ways to increase their influence for God.

A warning must be considered. Most pastors easily discern God's fulfillment in their yesterdays, but they struggle about today. Why not watch carefully for God in your present moments instead of working so hard to sharpen your 20/20 hindsight? Why not turn today's troublesome circumstances into magnificent fulfillment? Spectacular blooming often depends on how we choose.

UNDERSTAND YOUR IMPORTANCE

God needs you now more than ever. The human race cannot afford to lose one more committed pastor. Without the salt of your ministry, society could putrefy. Without your light, the darkness could grow blacker still.

As we discussed in our earlier book, *Pastors at Risk*, pastors going AWOL has increased and everyone admits the parish ministry is harder now than it once was. The mind-boggling causes include membership migration, distracted church members, declining moral absolutes and unrealistic expectations from many sources. The resulting moral decline in our society makes ministry difficult, but you are desperately needed.

Tony Snow, a *Detroit News* columnist, sounds like a modern prophet: "While activists and judges have shoved religion from the public stage, usually under the guise of separating church and state, religious figures have made the task easy. They have committed the cardinal mistake of snuggling too close to power and submitting to compromises that have bought them respectability without earning them respect."[6]

Although these current days confuse us, we may be the only hope for faith, righteousness and truth to be rechiseled into society's psyche. We must recognize how much our troubled world needs us.

Society Has Many Problems
Let's admit that no one knows how to deal with the moral decay and spiritual disintegration sweeping our nation and world. A serious sickness of

the soul seems to be crippling individuals, families, churches and communities. Counterfeit ministries have nauseated the masses. Judeo-Christian
values are being discarded without trial. Something must be done.

Civilization stands at a moral abyss. Nearly every day the media
reports some new degeneracy that is spreading in epidemic proportions.
Newscasters, sounding like Old Testament holy men using newfangled
technology, predict that doomsday is just around the corner.

Without intending to be religious, they remind us constantly that we
are being destroyed, like the Roman Empire, from within. Chastity and
character have fallen to a low ebb. Rooted in a permissive revolution,
family, home and society are reaping a toxic harvest. Although moderns
call it social blight, earlier generations called it sin. And that's what it is.

Children are also at risk. Dr. James Dobson, founder and president of
Focus on the Family, and Gary Bauer, president of the Family Research
Council in Washington, D.C., summarize the current situation:

> America is involved in a second civil war. On one side are
> those who defend family, faith and traditional values. On the
> other side are those who aggressively reject any hint of tra-
> dition or religion and want a society based on secular values.
> Both value systems cannot co-exist. One will prevail. And the
> one that survives will control the hearts and minds of
> America's children. The younger generation is already suffer-
> ing. Drugs, value-free education, youth suicide, crime, homo-
> sexuality...all are taking a terrible toll. Many Americans know
> their kids are hurting, but they may not comprehend what
> has gone wrong.[7]

William Raspberry, a *Washington Post* columnist, explains the frightening and corrupt jungle children are forced to live in: "We're raising up a
generation of youngsters who are numb to violence and hatred, who
know death at close hand and who seriously doubt, as children never
should, that they will survive to reach adulthood and middle age.
Joblessness, hopelessness, miseducation, family deterioration, erosion of
fundamental values—all these things contribute to our children's loss of

innocence."[8] It sounds like a society that needs the Church and our ministry more than ever.

Churches Often Reflect Culture

To make matters worse, the church in many places has allowed itself to become a sickening reflection of the prevailing culture. In a 1993 issue, *Newsweek* called it the "Dead End of Mainlines," where established

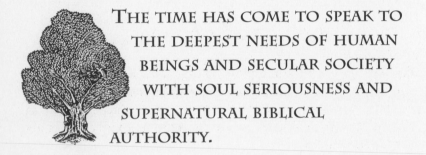

THE TIME HAS COME TO SPEAK TO THE DEEPEST NEEDS OF HUMAN BEINGS AND SECULAR SOCIETY WITH SOUL SERIOUSNESS AND SUPERNATURAL BIBLICAL AUTHORITY.

churches have overdosed on trendy theology, created a moral blur and are now worried sick about shrinking memberships and income.[9]

Consequently, the Church's voice is either silent or feebly raised in protest against symptoms rather than causes. Like a sinking *Titanic*, timeless values of Christianity are being abandoned. Almost spiritually bankrupt, these churches can no longer legitimately consider themselves a redemptive alien in a society they helped secularize.

In light of these realities, it's much too late for more opinion polls and focus groups and national conferences to speculate about morality and faith and righteousness. The time has come to speak to the deepest needs of human beings and secular society with soul seriousness and supernatural biblical authority.

A miraculous spiritual revolution is needed to clean up the immoral cesspool that is drowning us. We must intercede for an awakening. We must speak of the gospel again with a supernatural anointing.

This cannot be accomplished by ministers who give up a day too soon, by those who suffer from professional inferiority complexes or by those who turn and run at the first sign of formidable opposition. Who will give our neighbors God's good news about forgiveness and grace and reconciliation if we don't? This is what God trusts us to do for our drifting society.

The power to alleviate this darkness is in our hearts and in our hands. We can light the lamps, stay the course and stop cursing the darkness. The fact that the world needs us so urgently makes it possible for us to bloom in lots of dark places.

USE CHANGE CREATIVELY

Like a raging river overflowing at flood stage, everything is changing. It can't be stopped. Old assumptions are being challenged and forsaken. Everything is heading downstream at a mind-boggling speed to an unknown destination. And every local congregation stands in the center of this pandemonium.

Leadership shifts, member migrations, economic upheavals and doctrinal dilutions multiply congregational changes. No congregation, regardless of how it resists change, is the same as it was—even as it was last year.

Some People Applaud Change

Ministers sometimes mistakenly begin a pastorate with the assumption that the entire congregation has its heels dug in against change. This is not always the case. Sprinkled throughout many churches are allies waiting for progressive signs from the top of the organization.

Despite their stick-in-the-mud reputations, congregations are no longer rigidly unchangeable, even when they want to be. Thus, a pastor should learn to manage change, understand that many people resist it out of fear and be aware that others welcome it as progress.

A wise old whittler who purposely impresses tourists as he kills time in a hotel lobby at Fairplay, Colorado, recently observed, "You better learn to like change because life is just one miserable change after another." He is correct. The question is not if the Church will change, but how? The real issues are: Change for what? Change to what? And how will change impact Kingdom work?

Use Imagination and Innovation

Any pastor who wishes to constructively use change must possess a pure character and use creative imagination. Warren Bennis, a management specialist and professor of business administration at the University of Southern California, offers wise counsel: "Positive change requires trust, clarity and participation. At this juncture in our world, all three seem as distant as Jupiter. But we have reached Jupiter, and so perhaps we can finally reach ourselves."

Bennis's next sentence offers extraordinary challenge for pastors, "Only people with virtue and vision can lead us out of this bog and back to high ground."[10] But in this whirlwind, the changeless components of the Christian gospel must be conserved and communicated in ways understandable to contemporary people.

However, a gale warning must be posted in every pastor's thought processes. Novel change is not the same as needed change. Ministers must resist the temptation to become what one bishop observed, "I know a pastor who is an apostle of change for no reason." Change for its own sake sometimes destroys a church.

As an example, the pastor of a 125-member northern California church instituted change because he wanted to be known as a nonconformist. So he moved the pulpit to a closet, declaring, "Jesus never used a pulpit."

He called hymnals relics. He preached from a controversial Bible translation because "it was not like the Bible my grandfather used." He strummed his guitar as the congregation sang from handmade overheads that were hard to read in broad daylight. He refused to take public offerings and asked people to place their gifts in a box at the rear of the sanctuary. He altered the starting time of the morning worship service.

When he announced organ music was out of date for modern praise services, he hardened resistance even more. When asked about these rapid changes, he replied, "Tradition kills churches." Much to his surprise, he was forced to move when his compulsions about change killed his leadership.

If a church is to bloom, change must be used creatively to improve ministry for those who currently attend and to expand the church's impact on secular people who don't attend. Whether you love or loathe change, the writer of the song "Be Still, My Soul" offers this assurance, "In every change He faithful will remain."

FOCUS ON A BIBLICAL MISSION

Define ministry accurately and clearly. Sharpen your perspective through Scripture, church history, believers and fellow ministers. Know what the target is. Check the promises again. Then, intentionally implement Christ's mandate in your ministry.

A clearly understood biblical mission keeps a church from being side-tracked. It helps a pastor create vision. It can produce such high motivation for genuine achievement that people can't be stopped from doing what they believe to be God's will for their church.

Many crises in troubled congregations whirl around misunderstandings concerning the Church's mission in our kind of world. A confused congregation led by a perplexed pastor never knows if it accomplishes anything worthwhile. The fundamental question is this: Does anyone have a clue about what the Church should be and do now?

An Uncertain Purpose Always Hinders
Confusion about purpose has lots of jumbled roots. Bizarre and informed voices, outside and inside our congregations, offer unsolicited opinions about the Church's task in the world. Some suggestions are extremely contradictory to biblical instruction.

The confusion deepens even more when alien groups such as gay activists and secular media experts tell the Church what her duty is, while branding her members as crackpots and hatemongers. The *Washington Post*, in a front-page story by Michael Weisskopf, referred to the so-called religious right as "largely poor, uneducated and easy to command."[11]

Another confusion arises when we use ministry as a label for too wide a range of church activities. These days, the designation "ministry" is applied to everything from rock music to abortion fights to basketball leagues to financial seminars to dinner parties to women's rights. This tendency to define ministry so broadly dilutes the Church's ability to focus on her objectives.

As a partial solution, a minister must know what business the church is in and must frequently communicate these priorities to the congregation. Without such understanding, a church may become bogged down

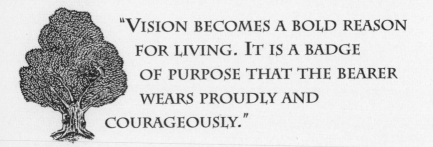

"VISION BECOMES A BOLD REASON FOR LIVING. IT IS A BADGE OF PURPOSE THAT THE BEARER WEARS PROUDLY AND COURAGEOUSLY."

in minutiae or overextended in nonproductive activities. Regrettably, when a church does not understand her reason for being, she vacillates into ingrown mediocrity or paralyzing apathy.

But do pastors know what the Church's mission is? It might be frightening to discover how few of us are able to accurately articulate the Church's mission. The Church loses her unique role in her members' lives and in society when she can't decide what is holy, ethical and first in priority.

Without a clear focus, ministry activity is often done at the margins of life. As a result, too much concentration is placed on peripheral issues. Consequently, entire centers of contemporary life are untouched by the transforming power of the gospel.

Vision and Mission Can Be Clear

To focus and clarify mission, the pastor must ask and answer several weighty questions. What is the essential core of modern ministry? What principles endure in every generation? Who sets the agenda? What criteria will we use to determine success? Such a focus-clarifying process can be shared among lay leaders, church members and the pastor. In this effort, keep remembering that congregations never rally to battle cries they do not hear.

The energy of a clarified mission to inspire you and your church is highlighted in George Barna's statement, "Vision becomes a bold reason for living. It is a badge of purpose that the bearer wears proudly and courageously."[12] He continues, "Vision is a means of describing the activity and development of the ministry, the way ministry will become more significant in the lives of people."[13]

UTILIZE THE PRESENT FULLY

History, heritage and tradition are important cornerstones of contemporary Christianity. As an inspirational way to recall God's faithfulness and to celebrate the courage of her pioneers, the Church loves to sing and to discuss her victorious yesterdays.

But nostalgia can be lethal and deadly when it encourages us to ignore present possibilities or keeps us from a wholehearted commitment to serve this present age. Something in us always stagnates when we disregard the present, fear the future or canonize the past.

Martin Luther changed his world and earned his well-deserved place in history when he seized the challenges of his current moment. John Knox, John Wesley, Dwight Moody, Billy Graham and other gospel greats did—and are doing—the same.

It is important to notice that while these heroes of the faith used their past to inform their present, they also modeled how each new generation should courageously apply the gospel to present possibilities.

Make the Gospel Real
Some of the most productive expressions of ministry in the Church's long pilgrimage of faith should be happening today. This is the precise reason why a pastor cannot pitch his tent in the past, misuse the present or resist the future. God wants us to make the gospel real in contemporary life.

Pastors sometimes waste years, waiting for something special to happen for them. In their imagination, the future is wrapped in flimsy ambition or airy fantasy. As a consequence, they never fully live in the present. So while waiting for some nebulous something, present ministry passes them by. They overlook the obvious fact that every effort, every expression of ministry and every new skill helps improve the future.

Another squandering of present opportunities occurs when a pastor gives more time and thought to church politics than to proficient ministerial competence. Everyone, especially the pastor, loses when that happens. Although no one denies political realities are at work in congregations, denominations and parachurch organizations, political maneuvering never saved one soul, fed a homeless child or gladdened the heart of God.

On the contrary, political jostling often hinders Kingdom work. In the process, the pastor misappropriates energies and imagination that he could have invested in helping hurting people or in personal pastoral development.

Utilize Your Opportunities

Somewhere in old class notes, I jotted this quote from an unknown author: "Yesterday is a canceled check, tomorrow is a promissory note and today is cash in hand. Spend it wisely." This is good advice for a pastor.

Ministry never bursts into full bloom at a magic moment in the future when one has more experience, finds the right town or receives some favored advantage. Effective ministry does not start in the misty distance. Your current post has a wealth of hidden potential. Why not find it?

Now is a good time to push through the fog of frustration or self-doubt to a new beginning. Stop waiting and start blooming where God has planted you. Realize that a second or third or fourth beginning for ministry can be more exhilarating, more fulfilling and more realistic than the first.

Today is all we have, but today is enough. Start tomorrow's longed-for supernatural achievement today. Leave behind delusions from earlier years. Treasure the present and use it well. Cultivate your spirituality, stability and strength to bloom a supernatural ministry in your present assignment.

Challenge Your Frustrations

A newly married couple started their first church in a small Midwest town. After about six months, the young wife said to her overly serious husband, "All you seem to think about or do is deal with what the church doesn't have, and it doesn't look like you're enjoying it much. All of this seems boring to me."

No pastoral assignment is made up of all frustrations or of all satisfactions. Every pastorate has a good supply of both. Although Old Testament Joseph never conceded that his brothers did right, the mindset through which he viewed frustrations made a colossal difference in the quality of his life and the results of his work, especially during his years in Egypt. As an overcomer, Joseph enjoyed usefulness and serenity even during his tough years of adversity. Jubilant victory finally came.

Clarify, Then Confront Problems

Clarifying and confronting frustrations force a pastor to try to understand adversarial circumstances and peculiar people. Then, his feelings about frustrations and his part in creating them become much clearer.

To challenge your frustrations, try this: Question, and attempt to eliminate, at least one frustration every day. Ask yourself:

- Are my frustrations real?
- Do they matter in light of the big picture of my ministry?
- Who or what causes them?
- How can I minimize my smoldering stress points?
- Do my frustrations flourish in some climates I create?

A realistic response to this process gives us a more accurate perspective. It unlocks self-understanding and encourages increased productivity. In the effort, a pastor uncovers internal and external resources he never knew existed. And he learns ways to change his conduct and attitudes to minimize or even to eliminate frustrations.

Challenge Your Concerns
Why not study ways to blunt the consequences your frustrations cause? Challenge your worries about money, burnout, family or church members. Sort fact from fiction. The payoff will be spiritual fitness and emotional wellness.

Sure, it requires work. But similar to "no pain, no gain" in physical conditioning, effective ministry develops through facing our frustrations and dealing with them. Such a strategy also assists us to identify possibilities in the midst of difficulties.

Why not commit to the reality that something significant can be accomplished for God in every setting? When you live by God's priorities and overcome your frustrations, the odds for such achievement are always on your side.

Unquestioned frustrations hamper ministry the same way a crop of dandelions keeps a lawn from thriving. Help your ministry grow by getting rid of the noxious weeds of frustration. Look beyond your problems to your potentialities. Look at every challenge as an opportunity to emerge triumphant through the power of God. Remember, the truth of Romans 8:31 has not changed: "If God is for us, who can be against us?"

DO A BIT OF STRETCHING

The approval and admiration of those we serve can be humbling. Those we lead believe we preach better than we do. They believe we pray more than we do. They assume we study more than we do. Many imagine we are better pastors than we know ourselves to be. A peasant woman stretched St. Francis of Assisi's soul when she said, "We pray that you are as good as we think you are." Similar stretching capabilities come to us through our church members' affirmations.

Why not become what they believe you are through God's gracious enablement? Some of the most extraordinary pastors of church history were loved into greatness by their congregations. Then, too, this exercise provides an antidote to our human tendency to infallibility where an overblown ego needs more applause, requires more good news and denies any hint that something might be wrong.

For pastors to be what people believe we are, provides for us an opportunity to celebrate the remarkable empowerment of God in our lives and ministry. Dr. Hudson T. Armerding, former Wheaton College president, underscores this exhilarating triumph: "Of all people we are the most aware of the fact that whatever was accomplished was not because of us. But we are also most conscious of how remarkably the power of God can work in and through a fallible believer like us."[14] Such awareness allows us to extol God's grace while frankly facing our frailties.

To succeed for God where we know we have our great natural limitations brings glory to Christ and irrepressible joy to us. What a sense of thankful satisfaction comes when we hear people affirm us at those exact points where our weaknesses force us to depend on God most. Accordingly, the affirmations can be a stimulus to help us become the useful vessels God needs us to be.

What a possibility these affirmations provide for growing a mature ministry! They help us more effectively serve our brothers and sisters in the family of God and bring delight to our Father. Why not encourage your ministry to bloom by putting into action the affirmations people give you? The stretching will do you good.

BECOME THE CHANGE YOU EXPECT

Everyone recognizes that contemporary pastors face absolute confusion on many levels of modern life. Meanwhile, Christianity seems stalled in dazed disarray concerning mission, vision, priorities and strategies. No one knows what to expect next. But because God providentially placed us in a world hell-bent on moral destruction is no reason to slow down or quit.

You Are Needed More than Ever
In this perplexing period of history, you as a pastor are more needed than ever before to be a competent ambassador, a forthright prophet and a perceptive emissary of the eternal gospel. Times like these require that a pastor devotedly demonstrate the message of Christ in his own life.

The confusing contemporary situation requires you to communicate the gospel through every means. Although it won't be easy, it must be done. Such a mandate compels us to know who we are, what business we are in, what and when we are to speak and how to apply the miraculous cures God has provided.

You become what you want the church to be. What a demanding, mind-boggling challenge. It's an idea whose time has come. I must be what I want the church to be. Christianity could revolutionize our world rapidly if every pastor decided to build this strategic exhortation into his ministry.

Consider Your Potential Impact on the World

Think of the impact that approximately 375,000 pastors could make on the United States and the world. Think of the potential. The responsibilities. The rekindling. The energizing. The reformation. The hope. It could mark the beginning of a moral revival, a new reign of righteousness and even the preservation of our civilization.

With apology to John W. Gardner, former secretary of Health, Education and Welfare and author of the book *On Leadership*, the following paragraphs paraphrase a "become the change you want to see" for pastors:

YOU can have a significant role in re-creating the state of the Church.

YOU can become symbols of moral purity in our society.

YOU can express biblical values that make the Church great and allow her to redemptively impact the culture.

Most importantly, YOU can conceive and articulate goals that lift people out of petty preoccupations, carry them above the conflicts that tear a church and society apart and unite them in pursuit of objectives worthy of their best efforts.[15]

God has sounded a solemn wake-up call. The message is as clear as the morning sun. In this baffling epoch of human history, He needs us to be strong and courageous and effective. The Church—a vital, living, changing entity—is susceptible to rotting decay or open to revolutionary renewal. What she becomes depends on us.

This is the time to energize one church at a time—your church. This is the time to spiritually overhaul one pastor at a time—you. This is the time to pay any price to make ministry so ablaze with God's presence that perplexed, broken people will be drawn to your church and be transformed one at a time.

Bloom where God has planted you.

CONTEMPORARY CHALLENGE
HOW TO BLOOM IN YOUR MINISTRY

- Take the gospel to the cutting edges of contemporary life.
- See your church as a living cell of the everlasting Church.
- Refuse to mark time.
- Reevaluate your opportunities.
- Find a cause that breaks your heart and then accept God's challenge to change it.
- Seek fulfillment as an intentional choice.
- Understand your significance in society.
- Define mission accurately and clearly.
- Confront your frustrations.
- Achieve your affirmations.
- Become the change you want to see happen.

Put yourself completely under the influence of Jesus, so that He may think His thoughts in your mind, do His work through your hands, for you will be all-powerful with Him to strengthen you. — Mother Teresa[16]

Notes

1. *Monday Morning,* July 1993, General Assembly Council of the Presbyterian Church (USA), Louisville, KY, p. 45.
2. Georges Bernanos, *Diary of a Country Priest* (New York: Carroll and Graf Publishers, 1937), p. 28.
3. Francis Bacon, *A Strategy for Daily Living* (New York: The Free Press, 1973), p. 22.
4. John W. Gardner, *On Leadership* (New York: Free Press, 1990), p. 198.
5. Ron Mehl, *Surprise Endings* (Sisters, OR: Multnomah Books, 1993), p. 172.
6. *Colorado Springs Gazette Telegraph,* Aug. 28, 1993, 15B.
7. James Dobson and Gary L. Bauer, *Children at Risk* (Dallas, TX: WORD Inc., 1990), back jacket.
8. *Denver Post,* July 6, 1993, 6B.
9. *Newsweek,* Aug. 9, 1993.
10. Warren Bennis, *Why Leaders Can't Lead* (San Francisco: Jossey-Bass, 1989), p. 27.
11. *Washington Post,* Feb. 1, 1993, 1A.
12. George Barna, *The Power of Vision* (Ventura, CA: Regal Books, 1992), p. 97.
13. Ibid., p. 98.
14. Hudson T. Armerding, *The Heart of Godly Leadership* (Wheaton, IL: Crossway Books, 1992), p. 202.
15. Bennis, *Why Leaders Can't Lead,* p. 13.
16. Mother Teresa, *A Gift for God* (San Francisco: HarperCollins, 1975), p. 37.

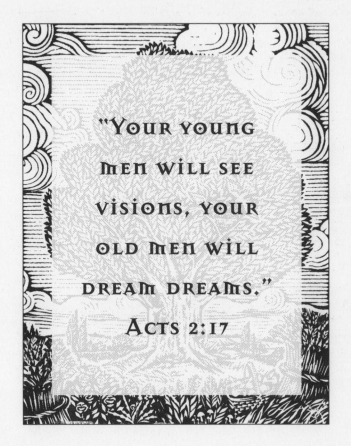

"Your young
men will see
visions, your
old men will
dream dreams."
Acts 2:17

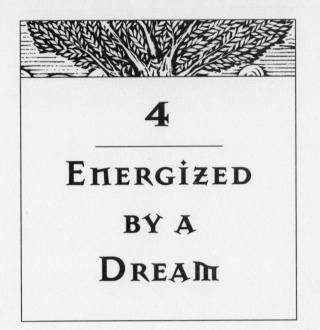

4

ENERGÍZED
BY A
DREAM

Father God, let my words be rooted in honesty
and my thoughts be lost in your light,
Unnameable God, my essence,
my origin, my life-blood, my home.[1]

DREAM THE IMPOSSIBLE DREAM

Dreams are the raw materials for adventure. They are heady stuff that enliven people and move mountains. Martin Luther King Jr.'s stirring "I have a dream" impacted human rights around the world. Then Irish dramatist George Bernard Shaw's visionary words still inspire the masses whenever they are quoted: "Some men see things as they are and say, 'Why?' I dream things that never were and say, 'Why not?'"

Joe Darion and Mitch Leigh's musical lyrics from the *Man of La Mancha* move us deeply and have added vitality to many sermons:

To dream the impossible dream, to fight the unbeatable foe,

To bear with unbearable sorrow, to run where the brave
  dare not go.
To fight for the right without question or pause.
To be willing to march into hell for a heavenly cause.[2]

A wise old preacher was right when he told two young beginning pastors as they walked together outside his retirement home: "A pastor never
achieves more than his dreams."

That's an important starting point for ministry in every generation.
Every pastor needs dreams that are passionately focused on the gospel
and its supernatural effect on people who make up the congregation he
serves.

Sadly, it is not always the case. "My dream is dead; I can't go on. Our
church services feel like we are tossing prayers into a wishing well.
Worship is empty." Those despairing comments in a recent letter from a
conscientious Midwest pastor are too common.

It's alarming how many dreamers are reducing Kingdom commitments
at a time when dreams and dreamers are needed most. The dreams Christ
gives us for our lives and for our ministry can't be allowed to die.
Something must be done to revive them quickly.

So much depends on the combined dreams of pastors across North
America. Think of the possibilities: thousands of ministers representing
an incredible force for setting direction, restoring purpose and calling the
world back to God. Think of the needs: perplexed persons, dysfunctional families, indifferent churches, deteriorating neighborhoods and a rotting society.

Superchurches, as important as they are, cannot do it all. But it is mind
boggling to imagine what could happen if hundreds or even thousands of
pastors started dreaming lofty, imaginative, impossible biblical dreams.
Nothing could stop such a spiritually powerful groundswell for renewing
righteousness.

Think of what we have to offer the world and how desperate things
are. Compared to Jesus, no one on any playing field in the world offers
a remedy for our moral wrongheadedness. Nothing but genuine
Christianity can redeem the souls of our cities, judge our widespread self-

indulgence or refocus congregations on the mission God wants fulfilled in the world. What an opportune time to dream, to serve and to become spiritual change agents. Dreams are the seeds of achievements.

Bring Back the Dreamers

Where have the dreamers gone? Are they hiding? Are they asleep or comatose? Who murdered hope? What choked the vision for the gospel out of our imaginations? The church must have more dreamers. What God wants every church to become must start as a compelling dream for an on-site dreamer.

Let's remember that every ministry started as someone's dream, including every church, parachurch ministry, church college, Christian publisher, missionary effort as well as hymns. That's the reason I (H. B.) love to dream about my part in the ministry of Jesus in the world. It is exciting to think that right this minute the Holy Spirit may be igniting a fantastic new expression of ministry in my heart or yours.

Dreams That Never Die

I find encouragement for dreaming about ministry from many sources. I remember my dreams being stretched by the lyrics of a song that still sings its way into my ministry: "The dream never dies, just the dreamer."

Let me explain the occasion, and the impact it made. Our church in Salem, Oregon, sometimes sponsored a summer series called "August Alive." The plan was uncomplicated. A different musical group came to sing every Sunday night during that month. Among the best loved of all singing groups were the Regenerations.

The leader, Derric Johnson, was a master at creating "aha" moments in the continuity between their songs. In one service, he described people whose dreams had died and whose aspirations had been crucified. He painted pictures of good people who have taken an honest look at ministry and have concluded that their hopes would never come to pass. So they stop singing, quit dreaming and accept the so-called inevitable.

In the same concert, Johnson told about pastors who stopped dreaming for their churches. He described how they gasp for spiritual breath because the passion of their calling has leaked out of their expectations and priorities. They mark time in assignments that bore them, though

FEW PEOPLE ARE MORE MISERABLE THAN A ONCE FIRED-UP CHRIST FOLLOWER WHO STOPS SINGING AND QUITS DREAMING.

they remember how it used to be. Hope has reached a low tide for them. Their vision is overcast and dark. Like the character in "Li'l Abner," they walk around with a cloud over their heads.

Dying Dreams Sap Energy

Such a loss often produces enormous personal pain. The agony showed in the face and speech of a pastor I know. He tried to plant a church that did not survive. He confessed, "Something in my heart died in that last service that I cannot describe. Oh, how it hurts!" Such grief for a dead dream depletes spiritual energy. Like the Psalmist, we wonder how we can sing the Lord's song in such a strange land (see Ps. 137:4).

Then, in the process, a dreadful reality increases the dreamer's torment. He cannot forget how things were supposed to be, even after the dream dies. Few people are more miserable than a once fired-up Christ follower who stops singing and quits dreaming.

Never forget the words of the Regenerations' song: "The dream never dies, just the dreamer. So come on everybody, dream along. The song never stops, just the singer. So come on everybody, sing along." That's an encouraging message for every disillusioned pastor.

Dream again and sing along. God, the giver of dreams, wants you to know that a new dream is the first step to conquering doubt and fear of failure. Our Father wants to ignite new dreams for you. He wants to reenergize and dream great dreams for you. He wants to give you impossible dreams for your church. In spite of limitations, God is able to renew your ability to imagine, hope, anticipate, expect and dream. Kindle new dreams in your soul. Remember, our dreams for ministry create a climate where faith and hope can take root and grow, for hope shapes the direction of our lives.

To get started dreaming again, try singing Phil Johnson's insightful song to yourself:

Give them all, give them all to Jesus,
Shattered dreams, wounded hearts, and broken toys;
Give them all, give them all to Jesus,
And he will turn your sorrows into joys.

Most of us have more reasons for dreaming than we are inclined to admit—a call, a cause, a commitment, a congregation and a world that needs us. In the event that these assets for dreams don't energize you, we have Christ to indwell us and the Bible to guide us.

Try Dreaming God's Dream Again
The contemporary Church is experiencing a frightening emergency, caused by a quiet but hopeless acquiescence to evil. The front lines, as in Desert Storm and Bosnia, are difficult to identify. And although the weapons often do not kill, they often maim ministers emotionally and spiritually for life. As a result, pastors' dreams are waning or burning out. The crisis shows in many ways.

My (H. B.'s) letters and phone calls provide me with a frontline seat where I see placid acceptance of the way things are. What can be done? As a start, every pastor needs to ask how God wants things to be, rather than simply accepting the situation as inevitable.

Pastors who visit and write to me at Focus on the Family talk openly about shattered dreams. The dying dreams show in weary faces and can be heard in tired voices. In their churches, the symptom shows in hackneyed religious phrases mumbled from hundreds of pulpits—words that lost their meaning long ago.

All over North America, you can meet pastors and spouses who have abandoned Kingdom dreams. Most are good-as-gold ministers who no longer have a reason to dream or sing. The quicksands of ministry have trapped them in a survival mode. They are desperately trying to keep their faith, their dignity and their means of making a living. All of this desperation harms their self-esteem, marriages, parenting and relation-

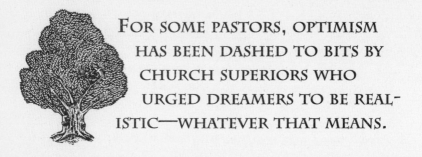

FOR SOME PASTORS, OPTIMISM
HAS BEEN DASHED TO BITS BY
CHURCH SUPERIORS WHO
URGED DREAMERS TO BE REAL-
ISTIC—WHATEVER THAT MEANS.

ships with the people in their churches and communities.

These pastors believe they have valid reasons for giving up. They speak about church controllers who destroy a church's vision because they cannot see beyond the next dollar. For others, optimism has been dashed to bits by church superiors who urged dreamers to be realistic— whatever that means.

Still others have had their high hopes stifled by church members who are unwilling to pay the price for spiritual greatness in the congregations because they do not see the point. Small, judgmental people have murdered the dreams of others.

The consequences should not surprise us. Their churches shrivel in spirit. Attendance dwindles a little more each year. And pastors die by inches as they mark time or quit.

Something has to be done fast. The incredible inner energy of Christianity cannot be allowed to be squandered for such absurd reasons. Seek a new vision for what God wants to do through us. Get serious. Get desperate. Get hungry and thirsty.

DREAM A NEW DREAM AGAIN

Start back at the beginning with Jesus. Invite Him into your situation.

Listen carefully again to our Lord's strong affirmation as if you were the only one to hear, "With man this is impossible, but not with God; all things are possible with God" (Mark 10:27).

That incredible, bigger-than-any-of-your-problems message was first spoken when Jesus and His disciples met a handsome, gifted, outwardly religious young Pharisee. Any pastor would welcome such a promising prospect. The young ruler, like seekers in every generation, wanted to make sense of his life. So he opened his heart to Jesus. Sadly, the man turned away from his only hope for meaning when Jesus explained that the cost of discipleship was not much—just everything.

The disciples were amazed at the conversation and its results. So they questioned Jesus as they watched this impressive prospect walk away from the Kingdom. "If this man can't get in, how can ordinary people like us inherit the kingdom of God? Who can, then, be saved?"

Jesus' answer speaks to every ministry problem anywhere. His words inspire every dreamer, even those with smoldering, about-to-die dreams: "With man this is impossible, but not with God; all things are possible with God" (Mark 10:27). The clear-as-day meaning of Jesus' words is that God delights in using ordinary people who will become fully committed to the cause of Christ. He uses run-of-the-mill folks like us rather than superstars.

All Things Are Possible
To pastors in every bewildering setting, our Lord offers these exhilarating, life-giving words, "All things are possible with God." That promise brings inspiration into even the most hopeless circumstances.

"All things are possible with God" brings hope back to dreamers who feel abandoned by God and other people. To those who serve in unknown outposts with limited resources, the message reminds you, "All things are possible with God."

These are God's words even to pastors who told their spouses last week, "Apparently God has forsaken this place. We're wasting our time. I'm sorry God allows us to squander our lives in this backwater place." Jesus challenges us, "Dream again."

A near identical message of hope appears in the biblical account of the young boy who was thrown into the water and fire by an evil spirit. The pained father was sure nothing could be done. So out of his own frustration of powerlessness, the father tells Jesus, "I've done everything. I've exhausted every solution. I believe it will always be this way. But do something if you can." The father added, as we might, "Is there anything you can do for my miserable despair?"

Then Jesus—Immanuel, God with us—answers as He always does, "Can I? You know I can. Everything is possible for anyone who believes."

Broken Dreams Can Be Mended

For years of pastoral ministry, there were many Mondays when I (Neil) wanted to quit. Often bad things rained on my plans for a spectacular Sunday of ministry: a key person let me down, the weather was bad, the attendance was low, a new convert missed church for the second week, three Sunday School teachers called in sick, the air conditioner wouldn't work or the organist threatened to quit. To add to the problem, I personally suffered from an adrenalin low although I didn't know what to call it.

During those days, I asked an experienced mentor about my feelings. His reply shaped my ministry, "I think it is God's way of keeping you depending on Him." Our Lord's promises are filled with supernatural sufficiency; "everything" and "all things" sound too good to be true. Or as one old-time preacher told his peers, "Those words are too good not to be true."

Then there are so many who quit really caring. Many just stop trying, stop praying and stop believing but continue their routines. They condition themselves to stop loving. One pastor wrote to Focus on the Family, "I hate to admit it but I just don't care anymore." These all-sufficient, life-giving words from Jesus are for those who used to care but have given up, "Everything is possible for anyone who believes."

Other pastors try to cope with these difficulties by saying they want to be realists. So they decide to take a hard look at ministry and to get practical about the future. Such a line of reasoning seems right and even sounds noble and lofty when spoken with a certain stained-glass tone of voice.

As these pastors look ahead, they see lack of support and declining confidence in the ministry. The fire is out. Ministry bores them. In a sense, their frustration is as intense as it was for those who actually quit.

They continue only because they do not know how to do anything else.

But a dead dream drops its burial garments and moves from the tomb to Main Street when one hears Jesus say, "Everything is possible for anyone who believes." These words from the Lord of life make broken dreams spring into bloom. This assurance helps us clear our toughest hurdles.

Attention, disheartened dreamers. Give Jesus your full concentration. He wants you to hear some important old words. Listen with your heart to two affirmations from the Lord: "Everything is possible for one who believes" and "With God all things are possible."

Did you hear? He really said it. Christ promises divine enablement so we can win over every defeat. Hope is then reborn as Jesus' words ring in our souls, "Can I do something? Are you kidding? Everything is possible with God."

THE MIRACULOUS POWER OF A GREAT DREAM

Everyone gains when a pastor revitalizes his dreams. He gains. His family gains. His church gains. His world gains. Start by taking Jesus' "everything" into your beat-up hopes. Dust off your unused opportunities with the life-giving words, "All things are possible with God." Then, ask God to help you see your assignment as He sees it. He placed you there because He wants something magnificent to happen there.

Every Congregation Needs a Dreamer

What does God want accomplished? Why have you been placed at this specific time in this setting? Why not return in memory to your original call?

Can you remember the time God asked you to fulfill impossible dreams in partnership with Him? Is it possible that your initial call included achieving something magnificent in your current setting? It's sobering to think that you may be the only person available and that you are the only person God plans to use in your particular assignment. It's serious, soul-searching business to believe that God wants you to help Him fulfill His dream for that assignment.

Let me (Neil) introduce you to some of God's unheralded dreamers.

I have in mind a young pastor friend in his middle 20s who started a church for street people in a Los Angeles warehouse. He serves people who find spiritual and social rehabilitation at the Los Angeles Mission but who have no church to attend after they leave the mission. As might be expected, the church and the pastor's family face severe money problems every week. But he dreams about the power of these resurrected lives on the future of the Kingdom.

I know a middle-aged Filipino woman in San Francisco who started a church for Chinese immigrants from the Philippines. She borrows a fellowship hall every Sunday from an established church in the Bay Area. She believes that God placed her there and that the future of the church is secure. Her dream is being fulfilled by the people who come to Christ through her ministry.

I know a beginning pastor who serves a church of retirees in central Florida. In addition to all of his other pastoral duties, in five years he has won 15 young husbands/fathers through personal evangelism efforts. Recently, he was invited to serve a larger church but declined because he felt he could not desert the converts. His dream is being fulfilled as these men make their homes truly Christian.

I know a pastor in his 60s who served a small church on the Navajo Indian Reservation. He earns his living by raising sheep. He serves on the tribal council of the Navajo Nation. His dream is to meet the spiritual needs of Native Americans.

I know a 35-year-old factory worker from near Indianapolis who, after graduating from a Bible college, planted a church 50 miles northeast of San Diego. His congregation meets in a school. He believes God gave him a dream to build a great church in Southern California.

I know a woman pastor in her early 60s who serves a tiny rural congregation in southern Missouri. After her husband died and her children were grown, she returned to school and graduated from a Bible college in her late 50s. When this rural church invited her to become its pastor, she shared her dream that she planned to stay as the pastor until retirement. Her dream is a church family to love for the rest of her working life.

God always has a plan for every community if He finds a person to fulfill it. The living Christ has redemptive dreams for Peoria, Phoenix, Parkersburg, Philadelphia, Portland—and all points in between. He has revolutionary strategies waiting to be implemented at rural crossroads, in violent ghettos and in well-heeled suburbs.

Remember, Jesus is the Lord of vital ministry for every setting.

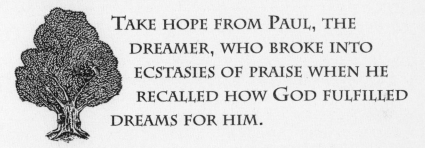

TAKE HOPE FROM PAUL, THE DREAMER, WHO BROKE INTO ECSTASIES OF PRAISE WHEN HE RECALLED HOW GOD FULFILLED DREAMS FOR HIM.

Resurrecting dead churches is His specialty. He wants to resuscitate dying church members. He wants to reenergize pastors. He wants pastors' spouses and children to have many good reasons to laugh and sing again. The Lord of the Church stands ready to transform dreams He gave you for His church into realities.

The challenge is to dream God's new dream for your setting. No place is impossible from God's point of view. Take hope from Paul, the dreamer, who broke into ecstasies of praise when he recalled how God fulfilled dreams for him. God helped Paul in so many ways, at so many different times, in so many impossible situations.

From personal experience, Paul knew how God rekindles hope and energizes dreams so ordinary folks can accomplish supernatural achievements in unexpected ways in tough places. The apostle almost sings as he writes to the Ephesians, "God can do anything, you know—far more than you could ever imagine or guess or request in your wildest dreams!" Then his pen dances across the parchment as he exclaims, "He does it not by pushing us around but by working within us, His Spirit deeply and gently working within us."[3] What a source of incredible energy for reviving dreams and restoring our songs—His Spirit working through us.

Believing and Dreaming Belong Together

I (H. B.) always have been a dreamer. I love to see God do impossible things. I have dreamed about battle-fatigued Christians and have seen God give them pulsating New Testament energy. I've grieved over split churches only to see God unify them in amazing ways. I've met hurting pastors and watched God renew them with nobility and vision.

Ministry for me has been a lifelong process of dreaming and believing. What an unbeatable combination. Dreaming of achievement, however, requires divine enablement; this is exciting and encouraging, sometimes miraculous. Along with you, I know I cannot do much in my own strength. But God is able to do more than we can think or ask or imagine. With God as the senior partner, a dreamer becomes an invincible force for righteousness wherever he may be.

First Steps Toward Miracles

Christopher Columbus dreamed a dream and discovered a continent. Beethoven dreamed how his symphonies would sound as he walked through forests and villages. Then when he wrote the music, it sounded exactly as he dreamed it would. Columbus and Beethoven can teach pastors lessons about envisioning the way things can be in ministry.

Why not dream something as stupendous for your church as Columbus dreamed or something as beautiful as Beethoven dreamed? Why not dream about taking the gospel to the cutting edge of human needs—way out in needy parts of society where the gospel seldom reaches? The world needs us there. The Church needs that. And that kind of achievement will enrich your life. God stands ready to respond to your dreams with the assurance, "All things are possible with God."

Einstein's development of the theory of relativity helps us with positive doubting. When Einstein was asked how he discovered the theory of relativity, he answered, "I questioned the axioms." His dream started when he questioned the way things were. He kept asking, "Why not?" Such positive doubting for Einstein became a seedbed for achievable dreams. The pattern that worked for Columbus, Beethoven and Einstein might help you renew your ministry to serve your present opportunity.

Similar advancement can be seen in technology, transportation as well as athletics. Someone tests borders. Records are broken. New methods are tried. Old ways are scrapped. People are retrained and morale is accelerated. Why not test musty old ways of doing ministry? Try performing ministry in innovative ways that will effectively impact today's world. Emphasize God's eternal newness. Work to see your church through the eyes of first-time visitors or prospects.

Resist Dream Destroyers

Strange and shocking forces inside and outside the church strangle our dreams for the Kingdom. Dreams for righteousness can die easily in a civilization that is hell-bent on dismantling morals and subsidizing behaviors that contradict our basic values.

Secular dream destroyers. Overdosing on sin and secularism and sex has almost destroyed our society. The list of dream destroyers in our society is frighteningly long—murder, rape, violent crimes, abortion, divorce, out-of-wedlock births, filthy television, vulgar coarseness, coldhearted callousness, suspicious cynicism and shallow banality. It's enough to make pastors withdraw in absolute despair, frustration and panic.

How can anyone dream God's dream in a society that deifies complex technology, cultural sophistication and social chaos while allowing itself to be governed by moral pygmies? Greedy materialism, secular humanism and godless paganism try to make us believe the world can be reformed without God's help. But strong evidence on every hand shows that this proposition is ludicrous.

Another downward pull in this society also affects us. Twentieth-century Americans have been conditioned by so many disappointments, we look right past the possibilities. Our culture seems infected by a morbid malaise of hopelessness, so millions fret about their jobs, pensions, old age and family as well as their health.

Therefore, masses of people, including Christians, settle for a way of thinking that assumes the future will be worse than the present. Half-truths are tolerated in the media and compromise is accepted in the church. We tolerate schools that do not educate, pay for medical services that do not heal and endure government that does not work. As we adjust to this corruption in society, we start accepting criminality, violence, illegitimacy and family breakdown as normal and to be expected.

Church dream destroyers. Subtle dream destroyers lurk inside church walls. In the church, dreams are easily destroyed by self-sovereignty in the pastor or lay leaders who allow themselves to believe anything goes as long as it sounds somewhat religious. Phony image building and doublespeak have become surprisingly common. Some pastors would rather try anything than do parish ministry and preach the Word of God.

In our churches, we too easily give up on the centrality of Christ, so we run our congregations like a democratic service club where everyone has a vote, where no faith commitments are required and where everyone does as he pleases. So much of what happens in the Church these days has nearly nothing to do with what the Church is supposed to be.

Self-sufficient dream destroyers. Dreams also burn low when we do ministry in our own strength. Os Guinness, in his book *No God But God*, says you can build a big-attendance church without much help from God.

He is right. Almost anyone, from a human point of view, can do the right things and people will be attracted to a church. You can grow a church numerically without God's empowerment and many people may attend. If you succeed in your own strength, however, your church will be a shallow, misguided, self-indulgent, muddled crowd that only faintly resembles God's dream for His Church or for your ministry.

By depending on their own strength, experience, competence and wit, many ministers undermine their dreams of accomplishing magnificent achievements for God. They forget that God seldom blesses self-sufficient disciples very much. All effort to do God's work in their own strength turns into bleak, discouraging struggles. Without God's empowerment, they become disillusioned. And they prove that Hebrews 11:6 is right, "Without faith it is impossible to please God."

Superficial results can also wreck our dreams. Pastors and church leaders generally agree that the ministry is harder now than ever before. This conclusion is accurate. Perplexing circumstances and low involvement by church members make the realities even worse.

A measure of the difficulty, however, may be rooted in ourselves. Maybe we do not give God opportunity to work miracles through us. Perhaps we have not allowed God to heal us on the inside so we can be wholesome healers for others. Or maybe we are like my 4-year-old grandson who said, "I can do it myself!"

How to Begin Dreaming Again

When will we say enough is enough and admit we need more verve, virtue and vitality from God? Let's follow our dreams and bring back resurrection life, personal transformation and holy living, although it has been judged as being unrealistic for moderns in many places. Nonsense. History offers examples of many pastors who dared to dream that God would take the gospel through them to change people, and He did.

We must stop asking, "Will it always be like this?" and change our environments. We must quit accepting as normal what newspapers, TV, radio and civic leaders say about our society.

As a first step, we must dream God's dream again for our families, for our churches and for our world. Kingdom dreams start with imagination and hope. They are fueled by faith in an idea, people and a specific setting. They are sustained by the enabling of the Holy Spirit. Let's begin.

Dream past your pain. The City of Hope in Duarte, located in Southern California, is a great hospital. I (H. B.) went there as a pastor on a regular basis. I visited people and observed what cancer and chemotherapy do. I tried to smile, hold the hands of patients and comfort them. But as I got into my car, tears often streamed from my eyes as I cried out in anguish, "Lord, it's not fair. These are good people. They love you. They are going to die. Why does it have to be this way?"

Please understand, I do not have all the answers for pain and suffering. But I know our Lord says to the sick and afflicted and to us, "With man it is impossible, but all things are possible with God." His words revive hope and rekindle dreams.

When any kind of pain and suffering trouble you, remember the Resurrection. After the scheming crucifiers did their worst, Jesus announced, "I am the resurrection and the life." This is a sure foundation for Kingdom dreams. We have Someone to count on who is absolutely trustworthy.

The kind of dreaming I envision is for us to rediscover the redemptive purpose God has for every pastor and for the churches we serve. I mean a dream where every pastor is consumed by a humanly impossible vision so he/she is able to dream God's magnificent dream even in difficult assignments among unresponsive people.

The dream I pray to be fulfilled is that every church will be saturated with resurrection power. I dream of a time when pastors will do ministry with indescribable gusto as they did in the New Testament.

This holy energy is undaunted by circumstances and comes from the full assurance that God is able to keep a pastor from falling (see Jude 24), to guard what you have entrusted to the Father for safekeeping (see 2 Tim. 1:12), and to do immeasurably more than we ask or imagine according to His power that is at work in us (see Eph. 3:20).

Dream past the enemy's lies. Satan wants to stop your dreams about ministry and personal spiritual growth. Your soul enemy, whom the Bible calls the spoiler, shows you awful mental pictures of the worst possible thing that could happen to you, your family and your ministry.

Satan knows ministry shuts down when he persuades you to focus on problems rather than on possibilities.

He paints the worst scenario for your ministry and makes you believe it will happen. It won't.

He wants you to believe there is no help. He lies.

He wants you to assume there is no hope for your children. Not true.

He wants you to suppose nothing can happen in your church. He lies.

He wants you to believe you cannot have fun in your marriage or adventure in your parenting. Not true.

Dr. Timothy George's strong words in a *Christianity Today* editorial put the issue in clear perspective, "In those times when we stumble for our footing in the awful swellings of the Jordan, and the Evil One whispers in our ear, 'Why did you ever decide to be a preacher anyway?' the right answer can only be, 'Cause I was called, you fool!'"[4] The enemy cannot be allowed to determine the intensity nor the outcome of our ministry.

We know the devil lies. He always does. Because we know who he is and what he does, why do we have such audacity in the Church of Jesus Christ to allow his lies of materialism and humanism and secularism to make us compromise our God-given dreams?

This is where we need to repent and cry out to God, "Renew my dreams. Reenergize my vision. Open my eyes to see beyond my circumstances to Your miraculous plans for me and the church I serve. Saturate my life and ministry with resurrection hope."

Such a renewed dream will transform us from sniffling weaklings to courageous achievers. A thousand difficulties may lie in our way, but God is able to bring us through. The devil may appear to have control of our

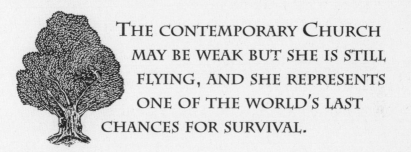

THE CONTEMPORARY CHURCH MAY BE WEAK BUT SHE IS STILL FLYING, AND SHE REPRESENTS ONE OF THE WORLD'S LAST CHANCES FOR SURVIVAL.

culture and the human race may be careening headlong to destruction, but the devil is no match for God. Beyond Satan's shackling control is the Savior's glorious sufficiency.

Dream past the Church's weaknesses. The Church is weak, but it is not dead. The Church in all her history has never had to face such a huge number of messy sins all at once and with so many weary, discouraged disciples. But God wants the Church to be robust again. This will require dreamers and prophets in thousands of pulpits announcing the meaning of Scripture for our time.

I love the story of the duck hunter who told his adult son, "I'm the best duck hunter in the world. And I am ready to prove it."

The son called his father's bluff, "Okay, Dad. Let's prove your skills tomorrow morning."

So they got up early on a freezing morning and went to the duck blind. It was wet. It was cold. Ice formed on their mustaches and their teeth chattered. The father urged patience, though no ducks were in sight.

Finally, one scrawny duck flew across the sky. It came closer and closer. The father took aim and pulled the trigger. An awful explosion followed. After the smoke and commotion cleared, the scrawny duck was still flying in the sky.

The father had to say something, so he announced, "Son, you have just witnessed a miracle. There before your eyes flies a dead duck."

The contemporary Church is like the scrawny duck. She still has life, but she needs reviving. She is tired, sick, anemic and confused by so many evils that confront her. She may be weak but she is still flying, and she represents one of the world's last chances for survival. A winning formula for infusing the Church with mission is dream + passion + priority = accomplished purpose.

INFLUENTIAL DREAMERS TEACH US HOW TO DREAM

Dreamers can be found on nearly every page of the Bible and in every generation of the Church's history. Most often they were unique in fitting ministry to a particular need of their time. But they had one thing in common: Modern and ancient dreamers all agree that significant achievement for the Kingdom starts with a bigger-than-life dream of what God wants done and then doing it.

Dreamers trust God to enable them to achieve supernatural exploits for the cause of Christ and for the people they serve. Seldom do they realize they are doing anything unusual in their dreaming and doing.

Moses Dreamed of Freedom for His Nation
What would have been the consequences if Moses had failed to follow God's dream? To inspire courage, read the biblical account again and let your imagination be staggered as you consider God's dream for Moses the herdsman.

Exodus recounts that while Moses was tending his father-in-law's sheep on the backside of the desert, God interrupted his entire pattern of life. The Almighty said, "Moses, you've done enough sheepherding. I want you to go lead several million people out of Egypt. I have it all prepared. I just want you to go and do it."

Like us, Moses asked absurd questions: "Well, Lord, aren't there mountains and water and sand that will complicate my life? Isn't it hot out there?" Moses never stopped to consider that everyone deals with mountains, water, sand and heat; many things we consider to be ministry difficulties are mere human problems that everyone faces.

God was patient with Moses and replied, "Yes, there will be obstacles, but we will overcome them together. I promise to guide you with a cloud by day and fire by night. I pledge I will be everything you need."

Moses minded God and led his people. Pharaoh was right behind them. The hindrances were bigger than anything any contemporary pastor faces on his most perplexing day. Moses probably would not have fulfilled the dream if he had first tried to figure it all out. But when God said it was going to be okay, that was enough for Moses. And it is enough for us.

The dream grew dim, however, as the children of Israel neared the Promised Land. Spies, who had never dreamed the dream, were sent to check out the land they were to inhabit. The spies were better at fact-finding than in faith believing. They looked the situation over and reported, "Oops! Something is wrong with the dream. We had better not go. We look like grasshoppers compared to those giants."

Can you imagine going through all they did to get so close to the Promised Land? Can you image so many people being frustrated for the rest of their lives because the spies never saw the dream? Can you image waiting 40 years in the wilderness for the old generation to die so they could possess the land God wanted them to have in the first place?

To modern dreamers, that means you should be careful who you choose as fact-finding spies. It means dreamers must be cautious about what they do with so-called "factual reports" prepared by those who never understand the dream.

We make the same mistakes when we let dreams grow dim or die. Then, we go through the motions of having church without divine enablement and wonder why it is so boring. Then, we languish near the Promised Land while we allow ourselves to be shackled by our excuses, prejudices and fears.

Sad for us and destructive for the cause of Christ—we may be only one dream away from a breakthrough. Much of the time, we stand only a prayer away from supernatural accomplishment.

What adventure we miss and what defeat we experience when we are frightened away from a dream by an obstacle that seems larger than the promises of God. Then, too, every dreamer must face the fact that every frustrated dream has eternal and negative consequences for someone we may never know.

Mother Teresa Dreamed of Compassion for the Destitute

Mother Teresa is a dreaming hero of contemporary Christians. You remember how she dreamed God's plans for her work for Him. She is a tiny, unassuming nun who grew weary of pointless activities for the Church. So she set out for Calcutta, India, where she dreamed of giving comfort, dignity and courage to homeless, lonely, dying people—not a pretty setting for ministry.

As an initial phase of fulfilling God's dream, Mother Teresa secured a small building in a pitiful area and opened the doors to dying, destitute people in Calcutta.

Mother Teresa's first patient was a homeless old woman, half eaten by rats and maggots. Mother Teresa helped this hopeless human being into her small center where she loved her and bathed her and caressed her until she died. That woman—and thousands since then—died knowing that she was cared for and loved. Everyone needs that kind of love when they approach the shadow of death.

In describing her work, Mother Teresa says the most dreadful disease in the world is not tuberculosis or cancer, but loneliness and not knowing you are loved. This little nun has given her life to her God-given dream. Her dream has miraculously multiplied so now thousands around the world help Mother Teresa fulfill her dream; some work in the centers, but thousands of others give their prayers, time and money to support the dream.

Think how Mother Teresa's dream impacts those she serves in their misery. Like ripples on a quiet pond, one obscure woman has challenged the whole world with an active new definition of Christian compassion.

As an incredible fringe benefit, her work among dying people has become a significant motivator to millions of others to encourage them to believe in their God-inspired dream.

Uncle Jimmy Dreamed of Healing for the Family

Let me (H. B.) tell you about an amazing dream that unfolds before my eyes every day at Focus on the Family. This dream astounds the secular world and inspires tens of thousands of Christians.

On the surface, the dream appears to have started in 1976 when Dr. James Dobson founded Focus on the Family.

But this ministry is more than the work of James Dobson. It started earlier in the heart of an almost obscure minister, Uncle Jimmy, Jim's father and my uncle. Uncle Jimmy gave his life to ministry as a pastor of small churches and as an itinerant evangelist. Later in his life, he taught art at colleges in California and Kansas.

Two years before his death at age 67, Uncle Jimmy had a beyond-imagination dream that challenged and mystified him.

Here's how James Dobson told the story on one of his radio programs: "My father was in prayer for three days and three nights about his own health and about the health of his brother-in-law back in 1977. Both of them were ministers, and he was asking the Lord to allow him to have more time, time to preach the gospel and to win people to the Lord; he had a passion for the ministry.

"The Lord spoke to him early one morning and told him that He had heard his prayer and that He was going to answer it. He said that He was going to reach literally millions of people around the world, but it was not going to be through his brother-in-law who had cancer. He said, 'It is not going to be through you either, but it is going to be through your son.'

"God revealed to Dad all that Focus on the Family has become, but my father had a massive heart attack the next day and was never able to tell me that story. My uncle died that very afternoon, so the story was not communicated to me until seven years later in 1985.

"My father had shared all of this with Alline Swann (his brother-in-law's sister), and she said she had wanted to tell me about it for seven

years but the Lord had said, 'Not yet.' In 1985, when I was going through
a really tough time (I was on the pornography commission, Focus on the
Family was going through some financial difficulties, the burden of this
ministry was so heavy), she said the Lord told her, 'This is the time.' So
she wrote me and told me the story.

"Then I realized, for the first time, why the blessing of the Lord has
been on this ministry. It doesn't have anything to do with me; my job is
just 'not to mess it up.' The truth of the matter is, the Lord answered the
prayer of my father, and that's why this ministry is here and why it is now
a worldwide outreach to the family. It is a gift to my dad. And the last
line of Alline Swann's letter said, 'The end is not yet.'"

Think of the faithfulness of God to Uncle Jimmy's prayers and dreams.
Dr. James Dobson, the son, went to Pasadena College and then into the
military reserve. Later he completed a graduate program at the
University of Southern California, earned his Ph.D. and served as a clin-
ical psychologist on the medical staff at Children's Hospital in Los
Angeles. He wrote a best-seller, *Dare to Discipline*, that helps families apply
Christian principles to their child rearing. Then one day this Focus on
the Family idea clicked with Dobson.

Following God's dream, Dobson resigned his position at the hospital,
rented a little office and began a modest ministry. His first radio broadcast was made in Chicago on the same day he had been beaten up emotionally and spiritually on the "Phil Donahue" show. Just before Donahue
and Dobson walked before the cameras, the host told Jim, "I want you to
know that I disagree completely with everything you believe in, and I
will do my best to prove it before this audience today."

After the television program, Dobson returned to his hotel room. He
stood looking out the window and prayed, "Lord, I'm embarrassed. I've
been disgraced before a nation of people. I am discouraged. And I am
supposed to go begin a radio ministry today. We have little money and
very few radio stations."

At that moment, God gave him a wake-up call, more real than an audible voice: "Jim, remember what your dad prayed. Remember what your
dad believed. Remember what your dad thought. The dream never dies;
it is still alive in you."

That night Dobson taped three radio programs, starting a ministry that reaches around the world. Uncle Jimmy dreamed for his son what he could not dream for himself. At the time of this writing, the broadcast is heard in more than 1,500 radio markets in the United States and Canada, plus several thousand more in 54 countries around the world. And the dream continues to bear unbelievable fruit.

Dream for Your Congregation

You, my friend, must dream for members of your congregation what they are incapable of dreaming for themselves.

Look in the mirror. You are the dreamer God designated to get your church dreaming and doing. He wants to inspire you with the miraculous possibilities for your church. Maybe you had low attendance last Sunday, the offering was down, two more Sunday School teachers threatened to quit, a key family is moving to a new job and the church facilities are run down. Maybe the situation is extremely desperate and you don't know what to do.

Maybe God wants you to dream your impossible limitations into supernatural opportunities. Remember, impossibilities are His specialty. Often they are the precise point where God inspires magnificent dreams for Kingdom achievement. Why not ask God to transform your worst hindrances into the fulfillment of an impossible dream? That's the way it was with Moses, Mother Teresa and Uncle Jimmy.

Moses' countrymen needed a courageously committed leader to make a difference. Often they had no intention of fulfilling what little they understood of the dream. But Moses persisted and succeeded in spite of their unbelief and stupidity. He took them to the edge of the Promised Land. On the way, Moses enjoyed seeing God's promise fulfilled—that every place his foot touched would be given to him.

Although the demands where you now serve may be confusing and disappointing, consider how much God needs you there. Ask Him for wisdom to lead your church to the cutting edge of faith and achievement. Try relinquishing your fear of failure and giving your uncertainties to God. Ask Him to give you a dream for your people like He gave to Moses.

Mother Teresa's dream sent her to share the love of Christ with the dying destitute of India. God assigned her to people no one else wanted to serve. The excruciating pain and terminal illnesses of these people would thoroughly depress most Christian workers. Who would choose to serve dying people who could do nothing for the Church, who could never give a dime, attend a service, hear a sermon, serve on a committee, sing in the choir or do anything else good church members do for their churches? Mother Teresa did.

Uncle Jimmy's pattern for dreaming also speaks to us. He saw a heartbreaking need developing in society. He saw homes falling apart and knew God was the only answer. Notice the implications for other dreamers.

God needs dreamers to weep and to pray about today's moral decay and dwindling churches. He is looking for faithful, loyal, listening disciples who open their hearts to Him and ask how to take the good news wherever human need abounds. He needs somebody to take ministry to AIDS hospital wards, to infiltrate gangs with the gospel, to homeless families and to other front lines of the war between good and evil.

Society needs ten thousand Uncle Jimmys to dream about how God wants the gospel applied to the moral decay that is causing so much havoc in our society.

What a collection of dreamers: Moses, Mother Teresa, James Dobson Sr. and you.

Dreams for Today's Pastors

Many other unknown dreamers are doing magnificent things for God. You may never hear about them because they serve in out-of-the-way places where they receive little attention in the media. Still, these dreamers are well known to God, and they impact many people with the gospel in incredibly significant ways. They depend on Jesus' promise, "All things are possible with God."

The authors, H. B. London Jr. and Neil B. Wiseman, dream about helping pastors bloom where God plants them. We view the local parish the way Sue Bender describes Amish farmers: "They make a lifetime commitment to the land, and their religious beliefs even determine farming methods. Over the years they have learned that with patience and perseverance they can transform dry, harsh land into a workable field. They have devised innovative ways to improve God's land...rotation of crops, use of irrigation and natural fertilizers, and the planting of alfalfa and clover all help to revitalize the land."[5]

It's a big dream we have for contemporary ministry. Some believe the dream is too big. Others believe the need is not nearly as great as we know it to be.

This Kingdom dream is to cherish and affirm pastors who doubt that their work matters. It does. Our dream is to encourage pastors with the reality that a supernatural breakthrough may be around the corner. Our dream is to inspire weary pastors to try again to make God's dream a reality in their churches. We dream about pastors rediscovering adventure in their calling so they can enjoy making a redemptive difference in churches, communities, countries—everywhere.

We believe God wants pastors to dream of saving the nation. We believe God wants pastors to dream of loving thousands into God's kingdom. We believe God wants pastors everywhere to dream of building spiritually sturdy churches.

Never desert your dreams. The old praise song, one still sung in youth camps, is still amazingly accurate, "God specializes in things thought impossible, and He can do what no other power can do."

Allow your dreams to direct your ministry. Focus on what matters most. Get fired up by what can happen. Tie your commitments and your dreams together so you see new ways of doing ministry. Take tenacity and fearlessness from T. E. Lawrence's poem:

All people dream; but not equally.
Those who dream by night
in the dusty recesses of their minds
wake in the day to find it was vanity.
But the dreamers of the day
are dangerous people,
for they may act their dreams with open eyes
to make it possible.[6]

CONTEMPORARY CHALLENGE
GOD WANTS TO MAKE YOUR
DREAMS COME TRUE

- Tough times require new dreams.
- Dreams always shape ministry.
- Dreamers find new ways to accomplish ministry.
- God starts every ministry from someone's dream.
- Faith, hope and curiosity are the raw materials for dreams.
- God's dream: every church saturated with resurrection power.
- Dreams are never achieved without someone's sacrifice.

The more we dream, the clearer our vision becomes.
—Danny Cox[7]

Notes
1. Stephen Mitchell, *A Book of Psalms* (New York: HarperCollins, 1993), p. 11.
2. "The Impossible Dream," *1001 Jumbo Song Book*, Hansen House, 13 Pleasant Avenue, Danvers, MA 01923, p. 208. Used by permission.
3. Eugene H. Peterson, *The Message* (Colorado Springs: NavPress, 1993), p. 405.
4. *Christianity Today*, Dec. 13, 1993, p. 15.

5. Sue Bender, *Plain and Simple* (San Francisco: HarperSanFrancisco, 1989), p. 63.
6. Quoted in Dennis T. Jaffe and Cynthia D. Scott, *Take This Job and Love It* (New York: Simon & Schuster, 1988), p. 69.
7. Danny Cox, *Leadership: When the Heat's On* (New York: McGraw-Hill, 1992), p. 193.

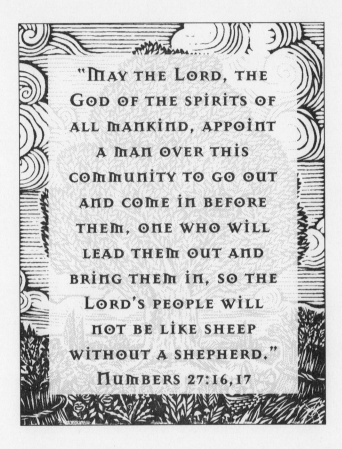

"MAY THE LORD, THE
GOD OF THE SPIRITS OF
ALL MANKIND, APPOINT
A MAN OVER THIS
COMMUNITY TO GO OUT
AND COME IN BEFORE
THEM, ONE WHO WILL
LEAD THEM OUT AND
BRING THEM IN, SO THE
LORD'S PEOPLE WILL
NOT BE LIKE SHEEP
WITHOUT A SHEPHERD."
NUMBERS 27:16,17

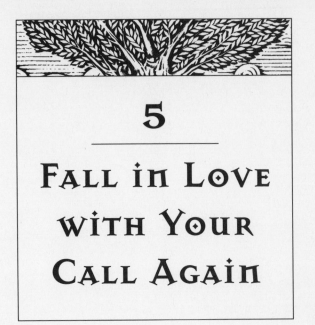

5

Fall in Love with Your Call Again

Originator of my call, reenergize my love for ministry,
empower my actions with authenticity, season my attitudes with
grace, and enable me to serve so others know Christianity is more
than a rule for life, but a Person to love.
Amen

Rekindle an Old Flame

"I have nothing more to prove in basketball," Michael Jordan said during a press conference that announced his retirement from basketball in 1993 at the age of 30.

At that time, the 6-foot, 6-inch National Basketball Association (NBA) superstar with the Chicago Bulls was considered the greatest player of his time, perhaps of all time. During a nine-year professional career, the former guard from the University of North Carolina scored 21,541 points in 667 regular season games for a 32.3-point average, the highest in NBA history.[1]

Jordan, who had been a member of the U.S. Olympic gold-medal "Dream Team," told reporters, "I've been on this roller coaster for nine years. It's time for me to ride something else."

Jordan's withdrawal has many parallels for weary pastors. It is frighteningly simple for a parish minister to lose his fire. Without frequent rekindling, passion for ministry may burn low or may die altogether. Problems quench the fire. Misplaced priorities and frequent disappointments dampen passion. Then when the flame starts to flicker, many ministers quit, burn out or drift into cycles of low achievement.

Unlike basketball motivation, however, a fervent passion for ministry can be refired with new challenges, worthwhile opportunities and a revitalized realization of our divine partnership with God. But beyond a basketball star's concerns with pay or popularity, a pastor deals with issues that ultimately count, such as truth, destiny, hope and faith.

Essayist Frederick Buechner's freeing sentence summarizes the amazing satisfaction a call provides, "The place God calls you to is the place where your deepest gladness and the world's deepest hungers meet." Relive your original call and rejoice in it.

A Call—Life Sentence or Bold Adventure?

A newspaper cartoon showed a large Angora cat portrayed as a presiding magistrate. To the frightened defendant kitten, the judge rendered his verdict, "Since you have been a bad kitty, I hereby sentence you to nine lives as a cat."

Ministry is frequently seen as a sentence that lasts for nine lifetimes. Many people think of a call as a judgment God uses to make a pastor miserable, to doom him to poverty and to strangle the fun out of his marriage, parenting and work. Nonsense! Why should ministry be viewed as anything less than an adventuresome way to live? Why do so many contemporary pastors sigh for something that might allow them to respectably leave pastoral service? Could it be that pastors themselves have lost faith in the importance of ministry?

The problem may be that our call to serve has become musty or dim or farfetched. Could it be that a frightening weakness of contemporary Christianity is rooted in this disconnection from our "divine sentness"?

Apparently, some pastors lost this inner spring of motivation years ago and never missed it. Some have forgotten how insistent the call was when they heard it the first time. Still other pastors question if a call they heard in their childhood or adolescence has relevance now. Most of us have forgotten the power of a few ordinary folks like us to change the world—that's our God-given mission.

A low-intensity call always leads to arid deserts of unsatisfying service, whatever our season of ministry. A disconnection from our call damages ministry fully as much as shutting off oxygen damages the brain or as withholding nourishment weakens the body. Ministry disorientation invariably follows.

On the contrary, a robust, up-to-date call energizes all phases of ministry. A call invigorates the person who is called and makes him spiritually alive. It sharpens his focus on the meaning of his ministry. It makes him more noble and more in touch with God than he could have ever been without it. It vitalizes vision and fuels motivation. And a call reserves a front-row seat for a pastor at what resurrection life does for human beings.

The God-initiated summons takes us into life's main arena where people wrestle with ultimate issues such as birth, life, death, sickness, broken relationships, health, hope as well as ambiguities and apprehension.

This partnership with God takes us to private and public places and to sorrowful and cheerful places. It is our lifetime ticket to represent Jesus at weddings, hospital waiting rooms, gravesides, baptisms, Holy Communion and life-shaping questions good people have reason to ask, such as, "Where is God now?"

A call to ministry supplies a driving force for ministry at the same time it empowers commitment to revolutionize the world for Christ. This God-inspired energy takes us to people who do not want us and empowers us to stay until they cannot get along without us. It is the gospel dressed in our shoe leather.

A Call Is Uniquely Personal
God's initial call to the ministry has very little to do with ability or skill or expertise. On the contrary, a call has everything to do with faith, devotion and yieldedness. A call starts most often at the core of our being where

God impacts our identity and self-worth, and it moves outward to the needs of the world or to a hurting person next door or across town. A call tends to clarify the meaning of our life and to give us a purpose for living.

A call combines supernatural and earthly dimensions. Those awesome words, "a call to the ministry," conjure up images of burning bushes and lightning strikes, but they also produce mental images of privilege and of being willing love slaves to the purposes of God.

Henry Nouwen, an influential devotional writer, suggests that at the point of a call a potential pastor "gets rid of the scaffolding: no friends to talk to, no phones to answer, no meetings to attend, no music to entertain, no books to distract—naked, vulnerable, weak, sinful, deprived, broken—nothing."[2]

This is a private meeting where God summons a person to a special work that he never comprehends completely. The call often highlights a person's weakness or failure so the enabling grace and empowerment of God stand out in bold relief in that person's whole scheme of living.

In the calling process, a person generally comes to view how weak he is, how much God intends him to become and how the world and the Church need someone just like him for this work.

A call means being used to impact a part of God's world—that noble and eternal part. At the same time, a call means I work where He sends me—in Fairbanks, Selma or Manhattan; that's the sweaty and earthy part of a call. It is a summons to unknown territory, but it always promises the company of the absolutely trustworthy God. It is realizing that it is more important to know who is leading than where you are going.

None of life's most lofty experiences for the called minister ever surpasses such a meeting with God. The called person can never forget the fact that he has been called. In a spiritual sense, his soul is indelibly branded forever. The Caller—God Himself—communicates a distinctly personal summons that can only be heard by the called, but he hears it like the thunder and generally for a lifetime.

A Call—A Love Connection to God

However, the love connection dimension of a call needs significantly more attention and visibility than it now has in most places. The ministry is love at work: love God shows to the pastor by trusting him, love the pastor shows for God by serving Him and love that God and the pastor show to human beings in need.

All the dreadful foreboding and enslavement verbiage so often heard about a call to ministry must be questioned and rejected for something better. Delight, gladness, pleasure, serenity, enchantment and also mis-

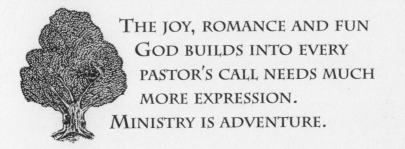

THE JOY, ROMANCE AND FUN
GOD BUILDS INTO EVERY
PASTOR'S CALL NEEDS MUCH
MORE EXPRESSION.
MINISTRY IS ADVENTURE.

sion accomplishment must be highlighted more. Glorious, vigorous "call to arms" words such as faith, hope, integrity, credibility and service must be stirred into the delightful recipe. The joy, romance and fun God builds into every pastor's call needs much more expression. Ministry is adventure.

I (Neil) met a newly married student who fairly shouted at the opening of our conversation, "I love being married. It's great!" His wife loves that kind of talk, and well she should. I wonder what would happen in every congregation if a pastor declared his wholehearted affection, "I love being your pastor"?

I met a first-time father last week who overflowed with enthusiasm, "Having our baby girl depend on me is the greatest joy of my life." That attitude might work in church, too. Why not start a revolution of communicating loving affection by every pastor in every pulpit: "Having a part in your spiritual development is the most exciting thing in the world for me." Think of the possibilities and spin-offs such a renewed love affair might cause.

A pastor friend of mine summarized ministry joyously and accurately, "I get to see more of what God does in one week than most people see in a lifetime." Our call always does that. If we are willing to see, it allows us to observe firsthand how people apply faith to the worst and best in their lives.

Let's get our bearings again. Our call takes us in love into the middle of delightful spiritual action—our own and others'! Ministry is not slavery but an agape love force for the spiritual recovery of self and society.

Unfortunately, for some people it is not enough to be anointed. We believe there is something better, bigger, more important, but in reality, the call is God's anointing. It does not get any better than that, but what more would anyone want?

A Call—Not Unlike Country Doctoring

To appreciate the amazing potential wrapped up in your call, try viewing your ministry as a spiritual counterpart to an old-time country doctor. The seasoned practitioner delivered babies, saw children through their growing-up years, gave them preventative shots, cured their fevers, listened to their dreams, helped them through puberty and pimples, taught them the facts of life, attended their weddings, delivered their children and then started the cycle again with the new generation.

"Old sawbones," as he was affectionately called, was frequently tired, frustrated by his failures, underpaid by his patients, poorly equipped by technology and not especially viewed as an important professional by his peers in big-city hospitals.

But as he lived his life, he had the incredible joy of knowing he saved Tom's life, brought Mary and her baby through difficult labor, sat up all night as Granny White changed worlds and prescribed healing medicine to make Jim feel better in two days.

The minister has a similar impact on the spiritual development of those he serves. He is a general practitioner, father confessor, spiritual obstetrician and faith specialist. Pastors, however, should enjoy much greater exhilaration than the country doctor.

They point people to Christ, enable others to make sense of life, preserve cracking marriages, teach faith to children, hold the hands of dying saints and share a holy partnership with Christ. The privileges and accomplishments are miraculous.

THE REALISTIC ROMANCE OF MINISTRY

Falling in love again with your call may be an adolescent, illogical or even utopian return to what never was, something like your first puppy love for the little girl next door or a crush on your kindergarten teacher.

On a more satisfying level, a rekindled realistic love for ministry may be more like making a long list of reasons to be in love on a legal pad after being married for a decade or even half a century.

Veterans of mature love in marriage and ministry say it is fully as sat-

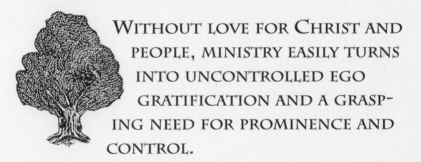

WITHOUT LOVE FOR CHRIST AND PEOPLE, MINISTRY EASILY TURNS INTO UNCONTROLLED EGO GRATIFICATION AND A GRASPING NEED FOR PROMINENCE AND CONTROL.

isfying as beginning love—maybe more so. And though some ministries and marriages endure without love, they are more enjoyable and more useful when fueled by affection, fidelity and shared dreams.

To fall in love again with our calling requires a return to the basic anchors of ministry. The pressing questions are:

- Who called you?
- Who started you in this work?
- How does love leak out of ministry?
- What will it take to make love your most compelling motivation again?
- Has secular culture strangled significance out of Christian service for you?

Love is the fascinating incentive for ministry—the exciting faith dimension that keeps a pastor's ministry personal and fresh and intimate.

Any other motive eventually frustrates and short-circuits ministry.

Love also provides a personal safeguard. Without love for Christ and people, ministry easily turns into uncontrolled ego gratification and a grasping need for prominence and control. Then a pastor is in danger of becoming a pontificating religious quack. Love for Christ, however, keeps us focused on what really counts.

Christ-closeness nourishes ministry. An example is an urban pastor who becomes dumfounded by the needs around him when he allows love for the Lord to grow dim. The needs are too vast, the resources too small. At a time like that, it is easy to feel rejected by those we serve and frustrated over their slow spiritual progress.

If, on the contrary, the same pastor keeps focused on his love motivation, he is able to see God working in even the most trying circumstances. Then he relishes his relationship to his Senior Partner who carries most of the load and directs his next move.

Our intentions and motivation are among the most important issues in ministry. Although pastors may be driven by many mixed motives, an authentic call must be rooted in a forthright commitment to serve God and a sincere yearning to care for hurting, sinful and broken people in Jesus' name. The bedrock foundation is a passion for truth, for pleasing God and for useful service.

Our task is to rekindle or to recapture the adventuresome love affair with our call that we knew at the start when God's direction was fresh as the morning dew.

Act as Though You Love Ministry

A middle-aged woman wrote to a syndicated "personal advice" columnist to report that after 25 years of marriage, she was falling out of love with her husband. She said the spark was gone, the glow dead; he snored and had gained 30 pounds. The old magic feeling had disappeared and she no longer heard bells or whistles. The children had grown and left home, so she lived in a lonely, empty nest. She asked for advice on how to desert, divorce and start again.

The counsel: Stay where you are. Start acting as if you are in love. Do loving deeds. Quit pitying yourself. Show love until warm feelings start growing again. They will. In this process, you might learn to love your husband more than you did when you counted on magic in place of authentic relationship, enduring faith and continuous loyalty.

Let's try taking that advice into ministry. Perhaps we could create an exciting, positive, self-fulfilling prophecy for ourselves.

A novice minister shared his dreams as a newcomer in an area ministerial association meeting. He told how he began his first assignment with extraordinary fervor in a place no one else wanted. He told about the futility he felt in his former occupation as a stockbroker. To anyone with a speck of spiritual savvy, his sense of call had the same electricity as Paul's vibrant phrase, "The hope to which he has called you" (Eph. 1:18).

Sadly, several seasoned pastors in the group responded with discouraging grousing about the monotonies of modern ministry. Their excitement had died; their focus had shifted to dreadful chores they detested. They whined about lackluster meetings, humdrum paper shuffling, fussy parishioners and self-inflicted coercion to succeed in a worldly way.

Understandably, God seemed far away from them and the people they served. They were spiritually depleted and felt no one received much help when they preached. Ministry was miserable, hard work for them.

The discrepancy these two radically different perspectives demonstrate is startling. The beginner is probably overly idealistic, and the veterans are much too gloomy. But the novice and the old hands need a mature love for ministry that can grow throughout a lifetime of service. Effective ministry cannot continue for long without it.

For many unfortunate reasons, thousands of pastors have lost faith in themselves and their calling. Therefore, if they are to serve adequately and happily in times like these, something supernatural has to happen to them. For their own well-being, for the good of the Church and for the salvation of the lost, something has to change.

Glory, privilege, joy and fulfillment have to be recaptured. The dying spark has to be stirred into a red hot fire. Duty has to become delight. Excitement must be revived. Love must be reborn. Imagination, intensity and anticipation have to flourish again. The first step, of course, is to act as though you love ministry as you did when you started.

Personalize Ministry Renewal
Every pastor has had a counseling experience with couples who seemed more interested in seeking a new love than in restoring an old one. The energy they are prepared to invest in a new relationship could rekindle meaning in the existing one. That same thing has to happen in your case so you recapture the glow and joy of ministry. When such a renewal takes place, you will never consider quitting to sell used cars, to become a social worker, to take up carpentry or to become a king.

Give yourself a reality check. You might already have more meaning

> GOD'S SUMMONS TO EVERY NEW
> GENERATION OF MINISTERS
> IS TO REVITALIZE, RENEW,
> REVIVE, REMAKE AND REFORM
> THEMSELVES, THEIR CHURCHES,
> THEIR COMMUNITIES AND THEIR
> CULTURES.

than you realize. No occupational fulfillment in the whole world faintly compares with the satisfaction a pastor enjoys who loves God, loves his call and shows love for the people he serves.

Few experiences are more fun than serving a congregation when things are going well. Nothing produces as much meaning as being needed. No other vocation allows a person to get so close to so many people in such life-changing ways. Renewing love for our calling takes effort and time and closeness. We all know that meaningful courtship always demands all of us—heart, mind, will and body. And this renewed love affair needs your all-out effort, too.

Remember that ministry is more than an honorable profession, a praiseworthy dedication or even a commendable way of life. Rather, it is a tender, life-giving relationship between the Savior and a shepherd.

Sometimes pastors believe ministry would be more effective and more enjoyable if systems, denominations, parachurch organizations or local congregations were reformed. Admittedly, some of these entities desperately need renewal. Remotivation for contemporary pastors will more likely come from persons than from organizations, from individual manifestations of ministry than from revitalized systems and from your heart than from your brain. Love for ministry must be renewed in one minister at a time. Treat yourself to new romance in your work for God.

Contemporize Your Message

"How could I be bored with my assignment when I look out on the congregation and count 25 baby Christians I had a part in leading to Christ?" is the way one pastor described his firsthand experience of this love lesson. He had moved beyond merely satisfying the saints into transforming troubled people. He quickly discovered that incredible satisfaction comes from ministries that reach contemporary people.

Each new generation must experience for itself the incredible joy of introducing its own generation to the gospel of Christ. Each generation must see this task as something much more than a dismal, drab exercise of conserving ancestral piety. Rather, God's summons to every new generation of ministers is to revitalize, renew, revive, remake and reform themselves, their churches, their communities and their cultures. Whatever its sin or secularism, each new age needs what the Christian gospel offers. When has the challenge to rediscover the gospel been greater than it is today?

The joy of communicating the gospel in terms that contemporary people understand will stretch your understanding of Scripture, your awareness of the moral bankruptcy of society and your speaking and writing skills. It has to be done. And the excitement of pointing secularized people to Christ brings new fulfillment and authenticity to your ministry.

Grow Past the Honeymoon

After the honeymoon ends, the house has to be cleaned, the garbage has to be taken out, routines have to be established, mortgage payments have to be made and the broken-down car has to be repaired.

Although no honeymoon lasts forever, love can develop into a significant lifetime experience. Although mature married love is not better than the first blush and rushing emotions of the first year of marriage, it is satisfying in different ways and is more enduring. It is not a denial of the joy of the beginning nor inferior to the honeymoon period. Beginning and ripening produce their own unique satisfactions.

A similar developmental growth should happen in ministry. After an exhilarating beginning when the pastor meets new people and feels the excitement of his education, ordination and installation, sermons must be prepared, sinners must be led to Christ, shut-ins must be visited, crises must be faced, believers must be trained, relationships must be established and money must be raised. The beginning and the continuing are meant to be important phases of the living out of ministry among the people of God. The excitement at the beginning was designed to be an important part of the happy process of maturing of ministry.

Even though renewing love for ministry and shaping it into a mature relationship requires energy and imagination, it requires much less effort than finding and moving to a new parish. This ripening relationship, like a maturing marriage, provides an additional payoff of a congregation of best friends who find and give strength to each other that short-term or superficial relationships simply cannot provide.

Like love in marriage, a ministry call often needs rejuvenation. One church leader believes that ordination services accomplish that purpose. He calls them "a time when veterans get to hear the recruitment speech again." He is right, but there are other ways, too. Why not search for maturing growth at every conceivable event and relationship in your pastorate? Cherish every affirmation parishioners give you. Look for it in every expression of service.

Pay whatever price it takes to find lasting satisfaction in your work for God. The resulting awareness of being on a momentous assignment for Him rekindles vigor, zest, mission, focus, dependence on God and affection for the work; it also strengthens personal spiritual stamina.

Nurture Your Call
Ministry is tomfoolery without a sacred summons. It is sheer madness to

tackle ministry without God's empowerment. But divine enablement is promised, and we need to keep plugged into it. In the process, greatness will be etched onto our souls.

But personal intimacy with Christ is our essential source for ministry. Devotion to God is the fertile soil where a ministry is rooted and grows to maturity. Without this basic bond, the call will be fuzzy. Thus, the call always gets out of focus when our relationship with Jesus is allowed to become ceremonial or superficial. On the contrary, closeness to Christ creates strong character and takes us to the center of God's redemptive activity among His people.

Ability to preach, knowledge about the Bible and theology or even ministerial experience are not sufficient. John Wesley's first concern for a pastor's intimate friendship with God should be ours, also. Before asking, "Has this candidate gifts for the work?" Wesley raised three prior questions: "Does he know God? Does he desire and seek nothing but God? Has he the love of God abiding in him?"[3] A call to ministry starts and can accomplish incredible achievement beyond our wildest dreams because of such a personal relationship between God and a pastor.

Although a call has far-reaching congregational and social dimensions, it begins as a private dialogue—an alive, life-changing encounter—between God and the minister to be. Although it may be later identified with a time and a place dimension where God met the prospective pastor, the call is really a holy meeting, an adventure with deity, an "aha" moment, an insistent urgency, a summons to active duty and an extravagant invitation combined.

One minister called it a spiritual showdown. He explained, "After being called, I felt like a marked man—no one else could see the mark but God and me. And I have been trying to work out the meaning of that meeting for a lifetime."

In the rough-and-tumble of ministry, every day brings some confusing events, disturbing ambiguities, wild fantasies or strange affiliations that team up to cause a pastor to question his adequacy, his commitment or his effectiveness. Although each new struggle may be slightly different, it is a struggle nonetheless. It is precisely in the midst of these questions and change points—whether they are personal, family or professional—

that our Lord comes and reminds us, "I have special need of you for a unique task even when you are at a high noon in these struggles."

Transform Concepts to Specifics

For some unknown reason, it is easy for the Christian faith to become a high-level academic pursuit such as the study of biology or physics— conceptual but not specific in its application to life's details. In moments of intimate communication with our Lord, He often brings clarity and concreteness to our attention. Then faith moves from the realm of abstractions and nebulous concepts to specifics and particulars. Then artificial walls between the secular and the sacred tumble down. Then radiant ministry flows from the heart and mind of the God-called minister who, in the quiet place, has received orders from the Commander-in-Chief.

The results: Ministry is clarified and prioritized, so we work with the strange notions, confusing backgrounds and infantile beliefs of real persons with specific needs. In this process, God helps a minister separate pastoral chaff from ministry wheat, so he is able to sort out which of his ministerial priorities and activities are for the glory of God and which are for the aggrandizement of his lofty intellect or conniving self-interest. Love energizes this give-and-take with deity that enables a pastor to make ministry specific for Jim and Mary, Tom and Sally, and Mark and Susan.

Ask God for Visionary Bigness

Every congregation needs a pastor to pray: "O God, our Father, let us not be content to wait and see what will happen, but give us the determination to make the right things happen."[4]

God wants such a growing edge on every pastor's call—a kind of fresh hope, a new beginning and a visionary bigness that sees beyond every limitation, whether it is real or imagined. A breakout spirit for every achievement for God is related to a pastor's call and is the only hope in many dying or dormant situations. In revitalizing one's call, God helps a pastor see what others might consider to be a lofty illusion as an unfinished reality of what God wants done in that setting.

This experience is similar to what a pastor experiences in his initial call when God shows him the whole world. Although it boggles his imagination and self-concept, the novice is forever impacted by a vision of global needs that someone must meet in Jesus' name.

This is exactly the situation in many struggling, tough church settings today. Something great needs to be done, and the only hope for super-natural achievement in that place is for the called one to believe God is already working and will bring significant achievement to pass.

This visionary bigness helps a pastor develop a clear, sharp vision for a given church, so he sees possibilities in a situation that no one else sees. This is how George Spencer was fired up to start his ministry. After fin-ishing Bible college, his call to ministry inspired him to plant a church among people he did not know, where the demographics were largely unfavorable and economic opportunities were stagnant.

He began working part-time as a grocery store bag boy in a tiny Oregon coastal town, making contacts with residents of the community. Six years later, mostly through loving people and after-school Bible clubs for children, he has developed a congregation made up mostly of new converts, has helped construct a church building on a five-acre tract of land and has won the affection of an entire community. No one else saw what he saw. He responded to what he believed to be God's specific assignment.

Welcome God's Challenge

A call always stretches a man to be more than he believes he can be. At one point in their training, Peace Corps volunteers in one location were assigned a 24-hour survival stint alone in the jungle.

One young man came away from the experience visibly shaken: "You know, as soon as I found some running water and got my hammock slung where I figured no tarantula would get me, I knew I'd be all right. But then it suddenly hit me: For the next 24 hours I'd have to pay a call on myself, and I wasn't sure I'd find anyone home."[5]

The invitation to ministry is a call to become like Christ fully as much as it is to do ministry. It keeps a pastor remembering who he is and Whose he has become. If we allow it, this process stretches us into the image of God's own dear Son and packs significant meaning into our lives. It may make us willing or even comfortable to be at home with whom we have become.

The call of God pushes a pastor to get to know himself. A college chapel speaker was strong on this point and urged students to heed this advice: "Know yourself. You size up professors, fellow students, girl and

PASTORS NEED TO LEARN WHO THEY ARE AND HOW GOD CAN UNIQUELY USE THEM.

boy friends; why not look at yourself? Meet yourself on campus and ask, 'Why am I here? What am I here for? What do I want? Where am I going?'"

As the speaker paused for a breath, a student in the balcony was heard to say in a stage whisper, "If that guy ever meets himself on this campus, we are going to observe the worst dog fight this school has ever seen."[6] Maybe the student was right about that particular speaker, but pastors need to learn who they are and how God can uniquely use them.

The reality: Because we never lead people to heights we have not climbed, a lived-out ministry call constantly stretches us to be more like the Master for whom we minister. The issue came clear in the life of a young minister. It happened as he was coming away from the graveside of a teenage boy he had just buried, when the youth's father said, "I don't know if I believe everything you said back there at my son's grave. But it means more than you can imagine for me to know that you believe it."[7]

This is the kind of stretching of heart and soul a call to ministry has on the pastor's faith and character development. God's stretching makes us better, purer and more like the Savior. The process reminds us of one pastor's comment, "God called me into ministry because that was the only way I would become like Him."

The list of personal stretch points of John Baillie, famous preacher from another generation, makes a serious pastor eager to grow beyond his own inadequacies into Christlikeness:

> My failure to be true even to my own accepted standards;
> My self-deception in face of temptation;
> My choosing of the worst when I know the better;
> My failure to apply to myself the standards of conduct I
>   demand of others;
> My blindness to the suffering of others and my slowness to
>   be taught by my own;
> My complacence toward wrongs that do not touch my own
>   case and my over-sensitiveness to those that do;
> My slowness to see the good in my fellows and to see the
>   evil in myself;
> My hardness of heart toward my neighbors' faults and my
>   readiness to make allowance for my own; and
> My unwillingness to believe God has called me to a small
>   work and my brother to a great one.[8]

YOU CAN FALL IN LOVE AGAIN

Start by believing in your heart that your ministry equips people to live a Christ-quality life. When you love ministry and demonstrate that love, your expressions of ministry impact people more than you can imagine. You will help people grow. At times you will swing from tender pastor to fiery prophet to pleading priest. You will enrich your life, too. You will stand taller and nobler. You will be more spiritual and less secular. You will have a cause to live for, to fight for and to die for. You will feel a sense of purpose, of making a difference and of recovered self-worth. Wrap your arms around your ministry, and it will love you back in ways beyond your loftiest dreams.

CONTEMPORARY CHALLENGE
WAYS TO FALL IN LOVE WITH YOUR MINISTRY

- Act as though you love ministry.
- Personalize your ministry renewal.
- Contemporize your message.
- Grow beyond your honeymoon.
- Nurture your call.
- Allow God to make ministry specific.
- Ask God for a visionary bigness.
- Welcome God's stretching.

The minister of the gospel is frightened by the magnitude of his assignment until he discovers the Presence at his side. —Milo Arnold[9]

Notes
  1. *Facts on File* (New York: Rand McNally & Co., Oct. 7, 1993), p. 759B1.
  2. Henri Nouwen, *The Way of the Heart* (New York: Seabury Press, 1981), p. 27.
  3. Robert Schnase, *Your Call to Ministry* (Nashville: Abingdon Press, 1991), p. 54.
  4. Catherine Marshall, *The Prayers of Peter Marshall* (New York, NY: Guideposts Association, Inc., 1954), p. 208.

5. Robert G. Cox, *Do You Mean Me, Lord?* quoting William Sloane Coffin (Philadelphia: Westminster Press, 1985), p. 26.

6. J. Winston Pearce, *God Calls Me* (Nashville: Convention Press, 1958), p. 25.

7. Cox, *Do You Mean Me, Lord?* quoting James McCutcheon, p. 24.

8. John Baillie, *A Diary of Private Prayer* (New York: Charles Scribner's Sons, 1977), p. 15.

9. Milo Arnold, *The Adventure of the Christian Ministry* (Kansas City, MO: Beacon Hill Press, 1967), p. 21.

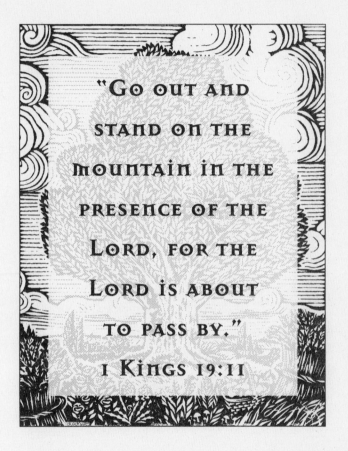

"GO OUT AND
STAND ON THE
MOUNTAIN IN THE
PRESENCE OF THE
LORD, FOR THE
LORD IS ABOUT
TO PASS BY."
1 KINGS 19:11

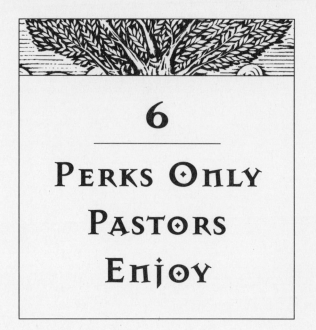

6

PERKS ONLY PASTORS ENJOY

Lord, I need You to help me to see satisfactions in service, to enjoy partnership with You, to delight in studying, seeking and speaking for You; and rescue me from the prison of merely doing my duty. Amen.

UNMATCHED FRINGE BENEFITS

Just now, the sound and smell and suffering of a hospital returns to me from an Easter Sunday dawn long ago. That morning, before I (Neil) went to preach the joyous resurrection truth to the people of God, the Father made me His spokesman to a grieving family whose teenage boy had been gravely injured in a car wreck the night before.

What glorious confusion I felt then as I observed brokenness and despair and pain and bewilderment in the hospital but saw wholeness and faith and healing and hope in the New Testament account of the Resurrection.

God's words for that family spoken through me brought them promise and victory—words I was incapable of speaking either spiritually or professionally. Every Easter since has held new meaning for me as I remember the holy anointing that came on my pastoral-care efforts that day.

I recall another time when anguish started to lift from a mother's countenance as she met me at her front door. I was there within five minutes after she was informed that her youngest son had been killed in a military accident. Although she seemed glad to have me there, it was the One I represented that sustained her.

I simply said, "I have come to cry with you." Then both of us were strengthened by the power of God's might in our inner person. As I recall that encounter after all these years, I am nearer to God today. Few people ever get to enjoy a perk like that.

Thousands of memories flood my mind when I reflect on the essence of ministry. I think of immense blessings and incredible perks I have received while representing Christ. I intend to stay in ministry all my life so I can continue enjoying these amazing surprises and incredible fringe benefits.

I love the privilege of living at the front lines of life where grace works and where the peace treaties of reconciliation are cosigned by God and broken people. As flawed and frail as I know myself to be, I am privileged to represent Christ at the main events of people's lives.

Outrageous Joys of Ministry

Unlike many church vocations, secular corporations often offer employees generous fringe benefits that cost as much as 40 percent over base salary. Such perks are costly to the business and wonderfully helpful to workers.

Labor and management leaders argue about who should be given credit for providing perks. Management claim that fringes started when businesses volunteered to share profits while labor leaders insist that perks became a reality only when workers demanded them. Whoever started fringes, the list frequently includes medical and life insurance, vacation pay, shorter work weeks, paid holidays, sick leave and retirement benefits.

Although pastors receive some of the same fringe benefits, their richest perks can never be enjoyed by those who work in corporate board rooms, hospital critical care units, courtrooms, or over-the-road diesel trucks. Like spring wild flowers, beautiful, unique perks surround pastors in rich profusion all along the ministry trail.

The possibilities of these miraculous satisfactions sparkle in C. S. Lewis's sensitive sentences: "Indeed, if we consider the unblushing promises of reward and the staggering nature of the rewards promised in the Gospel, it would seem that our Lord finds our desires not too strong, but too weak. We are half-hearted creatures, fooling about with drink and sex and ambition when infinite joy is offered us. We are like an ignorant child who wants to go on making mud pies in a slum because he cannot imagine what is meant by the offer of a holiday at the sea. We are far too easily pleased."[1] Those noble words make a person wonder why anyone would settle to be a king if he could be a pastor.

Faith Really Works

Some time ago, I led a funeral celebration for a 94-year-old believer. Until a few weeks before her death, she played hymns she had known since childhood although she could not remember her own name and could not recognize her children.

We had been out of touch for nearly 25 years, but I had once been her pastor. She had outlived her friends and siblings and spouse. Advancing age kept her from church for years. But I was moved with satisfaction by the imprint the songs of faith made on her soul. I was glad to hear her children and grandchildren and great-grandchildren talk about the power of a touch, a gentle word, a kind affirmation, a listening ear or an assuring prayer. This is a great perk for a pastor—to see what grace does in a long, holy life.

Her family highlighted another perk when they spoke kindly about my influence in their lives so many years ago. What a pleasing benefit to know our effect on people is more important than ticker-tape parades or tall monuments created in our honor. Our joy is people who need our encouragement, our concern about their relationship to the Savior, our prevailing prayers and our unique ministry.

Would you believe a woman attending that funeral was a church member I had loaded into my car on a snowy wintery night (about 2:00 A.M., as I remember) to take to an emergency room because she had overdosed? The doctor pumped her stomach and I took her home. There she was 25 years later, enjoying life, visiting with friends following the funeral and showing pictures of her grandchildren and great-grandchildren. Who but a pastor has such perks and fringes and blessings and opportunities? We enjoy sustained satisfactions no other occupation group ever experiences.

A Renewed Focus on What Really Matters

Many pastors these days are taking a novel new look—or is it a serious old look?—at genuine pastoral perks. More and more ministers are rethinking what they consider the most significant segments of ministry to be for them. It's a healthy trend.

In the '90s, spiritual leaders in spiraling numbers seek increased fulfillment from their marriages, from personal spiritual growth and from offering supportive care to people in crises. Faith midwifery of new converts is producing unspeakable joy for many contemporary pastors, as it should.

Increasing fulfillment is being rediscovered in imaginative life-changing preaching and in helping believers find a vibrant intimacy with Christ. Such an impressive perks list cannot be found anywhere outside a pastorate.

This trend means more ministers have decided to ignore trivia and to pay less attention to unimportant expectations from outside sources. They want to give primary concentration to what is essential. They define fulfillment on their own terms, unwilling to relinquish this choice of satisfaction to church members, to denominational leaders or to anyone else.

This new breed finds enormous contentment in making a supernatural impact on people near them. In the process, their ministry focus becomes more local than global and more tangible than theoretical. Many say they discover incredible contentment in developing the spirituality of others and in ripening their own faith.

Sustained satisfaction starts by recognizing the incredible perks God plants around the edge of every pastoral assignment. Fulfillment can be found wherever anyone needs ministry. And being a pastor means God sends us to those places often.

Satisfaction 1: Stress Your Specialty

It is difficult to fathom why some ministers are sometimes shy about discussing the most magnificent reality in the world. Edison never considered keeping electricity to himself.

Neither did Alexander Bell keep the telephone locked up in his creative imagination and refuse to tell the world. Or how would a resourceful medical researcher be judged who refused to share a newly discovered cancer cure? Or what about a cardiologist who declined to treat heart disease?

Neither can we keep God's good news to ourselves. It's time to overcome our timidity and take our supernatural specialty to the street.

It Worked for Ruby Bridges

Take the case of Ruby Bridges.

The story was recounted on April 30, 1993, by Dr. Robert Coles, who delivered a keynote address to the Provident Counseling Annual Conference in St. Louis, Missouri. Eight hundred professionals—educators, social workers and mental health therapists—attended the event.

Coles, a Harvard professor and Pulitzer Prize-winning author, spoke of the potential vitality of faith as he recalled how six-year-old Ruby Bridges' resilience surprised him as nothing else in his professional practice had done.

Ruby Bridges was the first black child to attend New Orleans' white Frantz School in 1960 when the courts ordered desegregation.[2] Although social scientists expected little Ruby to be plagued by eating and sleep disorders, she appeared to suffer no difficulties. The reason—robust religious convictions learned from her devoted Christian parents bolstered her. She learned from them to pray, "Please, God, forgive them because they don't know what they are doing."

Coles continued, "Ruby told me her mother and grandmother instructed her that was a fitting prayer. Amazingly, her petition connected her with something that happened a couple of thousand years before in a distant land with the life of an itinerant preacher whose name was Jesus."

As professionals interviewed the girl, they were surprised to find inner spiritual sources strengthened her and kept her emotionally fit, even at her young age.

Later, while discussing what every pastor knows to be spiritual

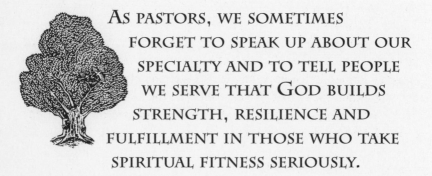

AS PASTORS, WE SOMETIMES FORGET TO SPEAK UP ABOUT OUR SPECIALTY AND TO TELL PEOPLE WE SERVE THAT GOD BUILDS STRENGTH, RESILIENCE AND FULFILLMENT IN THOSE WHO TAKE SPIRITUAL FITNESS SERIOUSLY.

empowerment, Coles urged conferees when counseling clients to "look within every life for the moral possibilities, rather than emphasizing dysfunction." Other conference speakers picked up the idea and suggested a valuing of "resilience and sustenance in individuals"—especially by those who have been toughened by trauma. Conferees, all helping professionals, were challenged to start using a new vocabulary of strength in place of depressing conversations about dysfunctional emotional illnesses.

These insights, shared among family therapists at the conference, sound surprisingly like the teachings of Jesus and Paul. But as pastors, we sometimes forget to speak up about our specialty and to tell people we serve that God builds strength, resilience and fulfillment in those who take spiritual fitness seriously.

Our sustained satisfaction multiplies as we use our grace-filled specialty to heal broken hearts, to mend shattered lives and to strengthen weak churches. Everything in that miraculous list deserves our best shot.

SATISFACTION 2: STRONG MARRIAGES ENERGIZE MINISTRY

Marriage provides an ideal relationship for a pastor to receive and give personal fulfillment and emotional strength. And 96 percent of today's pastors are married.[3] A minister does not work at building a strong marriage to make his ministry more credible or impressive but to make himself and his spouse more whole persons.

A starting point for ensuring meaning is to wholeheartedly accept the fact that nothing is gained when marriage and ministry are allowed to compete for our first priority. Ideally, ministry and marriage complement and strengthen each other. We can celebrate the fact that marriage and family are microcosms of the Church and the kingdom of God—a rich source for what is truly satisfying in life.

Young Couple Sought Help

I know a delightfully devoted young ministry couple who had a common, although mostly undiscussed, handicap that kept them from effective ministry. They came from broken family backgrounds, so their models for marriage were grossly flawed. To protect their identity, let me call them Sally and Malcolm.

They are two thoroughly converted human beings who met at a Christian college and married in their early 20s. At their marriage, they dedicated their future to serving together in ministry. They viewed that commitment as a privilege rather than as an obligation. As they took their first church, they looked forward to introducing people to Christ, to sharing ministry activities and to allowing their congregation to nourish their own faith. On a potential scale of 1 to 10, they are a high 9.

Without realizing it, however, they were emotional cripples. Both had turbulently dysfunctional family backgrounds, she from child abuse and he from long-term alcoholism.

Almost immediately in their new church setting, they realized that making their marriage strong had to take place before they could help others. So they took an emotional three-month time-out. They continued their ministry part-time, but the primary work focus was to find resources to help their marriage.

They gave it the same priority a family devotes to a medical emergency. During that time, they sought help from counselors, read books together, instituted a mentoring relationship with a mature clergy couple in a nearby town and attended marriage workshops. Eventually they were well enough to minister to others.

Similar situations are increasingly common in many ministry settings. Due to incredibly high incidents of family and emotional and spiritual dysfunction in our society, many contemporary pastors and spouses bring painful brokenness into ministry. In our culture, it is no longer safe to assume two spiritually motivated Christian people know how to nourish marriage or ministry for themselves or for others.

Sally and Malcolm started growing their marriage by leaps and bounds when they understood that a meaningful relationship requires persevering commitment and determined faith—something they never observed in their childhood homes. In the long range, their mended brokenness enhanced the effectiveness of their ministry to other hurting people. They became authentic wounded healers.

Couple Made Home a Sanctuary

Another couple I know used their home as a setting for a satisfying perk many pastors overlook. As a starting point for bolstering marriage and for increasing ministry satisfactions, this couple turned their home into a private sanctuary, a place of retreat and togetherness and solid spirituality where they could recharge their emotional batteries and could refocus their perspectives about ministry.

Both were involved in highly demanding professions, she as a high school counselor and he as a pastor, which kept them close to the emotional edge. Both of their jobs required immense psychological, spiritual and physical energy. So they intentionally used their home to enrich their relationship and to renew ministry.

In this process, they discovered that a good marriage for a ministry couple requires as much hard work as any other marriage, maybe more. The effort paid off, however. They made their marriage a source of joy and fun. They are quality people, mostly because they have a quality marriage.

They have learned from personal experience that neither marriage nor ministry flourish much when marriage and ministry are rivals. Thus, instead of allowing feelings of competition between marriage and ministry, this couple give high priority to their marriage—a strategy that fortifies and energizes ministry. He sees their commitment to each other as a source of strength for his ministry. In the process of making their marriage a sanctuary, they have "affair proofed" their marriage.

Marriage Keeps Ministry on Track

I also know a young pastor who serves in a rural church near Little Rock, Arkansas. I greatly admire his commitment to ministry and to marriage. He recently wrote, "Marriage is an adventure in amazement and ambiguity which, in some strange ways, helps keep ministry on track."

He is correct, whether a minister's marriage is in the youthful passion-charged stage or in a more mellow-violin stage. Living in a ministry marriage forces every couple to deal with the humdrum questions everyone else faces.

Marriage, especially ministry couples, can also enrich the question of meaning, forcing couples to deal with significant fulfillment issues that are spiritual and emotional such as intimacy, forgiveness, extended family, parenting, money, growing old, illness and even death.

To be an authentic spokesperson for God and an effective family counselor, it helps if a pastor has personal firsthand experience of humdrum demands and more ultimate life-impacting issues. In a "special gift to yourself kind of way," a great marriage enriches ministry, and Christ-centered ministry enriches marriage.

Marital Satisfaction—A Key to Other Relationships

Like an emotional or spiritual mirror, marriage shows us much about ourselves and how we influence others. It gives a pastor authentic clues about all relationships. There is another profound bonus to those people who listen to his preaching—his own marriage keeps his pulpit statements about marriage and home realistic and beneficial.

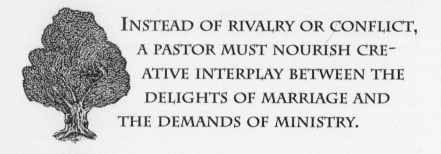

INSTEAD OF RIVALRY OR CONFLICT, A PASTOR MUST NOURISH CREATIVE INTERPLAY BETWEEN THE DELIGHTS OF MARRIAGE AND THE DEMANDS OF MINISTRY.

For these reasons and more, a pastor cannot allow rigorous requirements of ministry to undermine marriage even in small ways. Instead of rivalry and conflict between marriage and ministry, a fulfilling interplay must be nourished between the delights and demands of both. Such creative give-and-take keeps a minister emotionally healthy and in touch with life. Then, when strains of ministry come, as inevitably they will, a solid marriage helps a pastor weather every storm.

SATISFACTION 3: FOCUS ON FAMILY FULFILLMENTS

"Family feeds and complicates ministry," was a veteran pastor's summary in a series of family life lectures to seminarians. This is an interesting way of saying that God designed the family as a remarkable source of well-being, but we sometimes allow it to become a bewildering or even clinical jigsaw puzzle.

Simply stated, a strong stable family is built on a balance of doing for, doing with and getting the family to do for each other. The family of God and the family at home have much in common.

Family Need Not Be a Runner-Up
That means, a winning formula for family and church is for the pastor's family to enrich and enable ministry instead of being forced to take second place.

Paul Pearsall, a family specialist, underscores the benefits of family in these words: "Being a part of any family can be the most important privilege of being human, the most healing experience of being alive and the source of lifelong and evolving understanding of what it really means to live."

Then he added an introspective admonition, "But first we must learn to raise our families instead of our children."[4] To make this idea come true, every pastor must provide maximum spiritual and emotional strength for all members of his family.

The task of parenting runs the gamut of experiences beginning with the hospital delivery room: changing diapers, caring for sick children, keeping track of Little League schedules, corralling children for Sunday School classes, family vacations, first dates, rebellious teens, college good-byes, weddings, grown children and the arrival of grandchildren. This partial list of parenting adventures shapes a pastor's perspective about life, ministry and himself.

Living and enjoying the rough-and-tumble of family life molds a pastor into the kind of authentic human being who enjoys such togetherness. For example, it is almost impossible for a pastor to get lost in his work when an eight-year-old Little Leaguer pushes into his office with demanding questions about the next game, especially if the caller looks exactly like the pastor looked at that age.

A Microcosm of the Family of God
Family, home and marriage should be celebrated as the most abiding and authentic relationship of a pastor's life. These ingredients provide a human-relations laboratory that shapes and seasons ministry.

Therefore, a pastor's family is not a pesky intrusion on lofty ministry activities but a source of clarification and vigor for him. Home and family provide sustained satisfactions and help him make sound adjustments to life. Firsthand family experiences put the minister in touch with incredibly wonderful human materials for building a great life for himself and others. It is a microcosm of the family of God.

SATISFACTION 4: LOVE IS A TWO-WAY STREET

A healthy, loving relationship between the pastor and the congregation is not the only thing that matters in a church, but nothing else matters much without it. Sadly, a congregational environment that treasures soul friends now seems at a low tide in many churches. This is most evident in groups of believers who talk most often about love, fellowship and community but fail to demonstrate it.

Although they preach frequently about love and fellowship, many contemporary pastors do not view developing soul friendships with fellow believers as an important or enabling part of their work. Many want to keep parishioners at a professional arm's length as a physician does with patients or a lawyer with clients or a supermarket manager with customers.

Thus, a cut-flower kind of Christianity results in the pastor's soul, causing a fine appearance with no roots for emotional and relational nourishment. As a result, such pastors become private and alienated and lonely. They forget to apply to their inner development what they preach about nourishing relationships being an essential ingredient for spiritual health. Why not consider these scriptural remedies for themselves?

When locked into this misconception, a pastor feels isolated in a crowd and friendless at church. Then he misses experiencing the magnificent renewal, energy and healing that wholesome bonds with other Christians provide.

Surrogate Families Needed

In a society like ours, so alienated by widespread dysfunction and detachment, masses of people hunger for a surrogate family to which they really belong. They crave emotional support and spiritual sustenance that satisfying relationships provide. They yearn for acceptance and togetherness. They hunger for a sense of family and agape love.

These wistful yearnings should push all of us in the Church to recover what the Church did so well through 2,000 years of Christian history—be the real family of God with all the richness and responsibility that implies. The goal is enduring love, nourished by a common loyalty to the living Christ. Everyone needs that, and the Church can provide it.

More than a Business Plan

Unfortunately, in many situations the church has a significantly different focus from that of an extended family. It appears that the church is reaping a gloomy harvest from a popular notion that every church would flourish if the pastor were a competent manager or a skillful administrator.

This assumption, copied from the secular marketplace, theorizes that pastors must be skilled managers with diagnostic skills, dogged determination and business shrewdness. Notice, these characteristics are not high priorities in biblical teaching. In this ensuing, though dubious, love

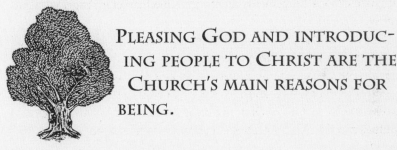 PLEASING GOD AND INTRODUCING PEOPLE TO CHRIST ARE THE CHURCH'S MAIN REASONS FOR BEING.

affair with secular management, the church borrows too heavily from business strategies and government practices.

Without thinking it through, lay leaders quickly pick up the theme and shout it to everyone who will listen, "The church should be run like a business." The concept sounds so reasonable that it has been put in motion on many levels of church life. Of course, no one argues against solid organization, fiscal soundness and competence in the church. But to make the church work according to God's plan, more is needed.

For the health of the family of God, His standards of relationship require more than sound business principles and prudent financial decisions. Hence, this crossover from the business world does not work well in the church.

The main difficulties come from the fact that the Church's mission is so diametrically different from commercial enterprises and civic organizations. Churches must develop people spiritually while businesses must earn profits.

These differences are staggering. Businesses produce products, offer services and meet competition. Government, although frequently off course, is intended to assist its citizens and not to make money; it is headed by those who seek reelection, who aspire to extract more taxes from the citizenry and who cater to special interest groups.

In comparison, the Almighty God is the supreme authority of the Church. Pleasing God and introducing people to Christ are the Church's main reasons for being. Contrary to standard practices in some places, the Church has nothing to sell, no one needs to be reelected and no special interests need to be served. The people the Church wants to win are looking for something different from what they see in the marketplace or in government.

Believers Bonded by Family Ties
To make the contrasts more distinct, God calls the Church to be His holy family. He wants this family to exist in a love relationship with Him and with each other. This love is not merely gushy or sentimental but an abiding affection for God and for each other, which helps a church keep her mission clear.

With this refocus on being the family of God, a congregation matures into members of a close-knit family who authentically care for each other. Thus, a church grows through relationships rather than by counting heads or dollars. Her influence keeps expanding as this love is lived out in happy human relationships. Expressions of this kind of love in a congregation make a church magnetic, especially to the lonely and broken. The family of God provides a charming attraction to the lonely, dysfunctional masses in our world.

This being true, a pastor must invest his devotion and energy and priorities into building strong spiritual bonds between people in his church.

This means he intentionally shifts his emphasis from being a church's administrative head to becoming a servant leader with a love for people.

Surprisingly, relations are often deepened at the precise moment a pastor relinquishes his management mentality and starts loving people for what they can become by grace. This challenge does not require a pastor to abandon good management processes but to infuse administrative duties with agape and soul and grace. It requires that good management practices nourish relationships. Everyone grows in the process.

To realize this purpose, a pastor must see himself as the head of an extended clan, something different from a CEO of an ecclesiastical enterprise. This happens as he establishes himself as a soul support to the friends of Jesus.

In this design, a pastor heads a band of brothers and sisters who become semifanatics in their love for each other and in pursuing the mission of Christ in the world. New believers then want to be adopted into God's family, and they are welcomed with open arms.

They become family—much more than customers or newcomers or clients. Precious babes in Christ are accepted into the church with much the same tender affection as one welcomes a new infant into a human family. The church then becomes a family of faith tied together by fascinating love for the Master and by tender affection for each other.

Jesus Showed Power of Love

Relational ties attract people who have little love in their lives from other sources, and this includes most of us. This plan to be a soul family to the friends of Christ is as old as the first century, when Jesus loved His disciples into the Kingdom and showed them how to love others. They were as close or closer to Him than family. He demonstrated before the critical eyes of established religionists and a surprised world that love is more essential than organizational flow charts or parliamentary procedures or secularized strategies. It has more appeal, too.

Love, acceptance, faith and hope were the glue that held the Early Church together. Their trademark was, "Behold how they love one another." Love for Christ sent them out to accomplish the most productive soul-winning achievements and church-planting accomplishments

the world has ever experienced. God still intends for love to be a domi-
nant source of sustained satisfaction for us.

SATISFACTION 5: CHAMPION IDEALS

Refuse to allow moral compromise or even the pastoral nitty-gritty to
short-circuit your ideals. Resist relationships that hint of thwarting your
vision or of undermining your awareness of God.

At the Bible college where I teach, we frequently invite pastors to
speak to the students in chapel. Recently a pastor offered this challenge:
"As pastors, you are the resident representative of the King of Glory.
Plead His cause often and well. Walk your talk. Allow the strength of
your personal faith to direct the details of ministry for you. An imposter
subverts the credibility of us all. And remember, one pastor cannot sustain satisfaction in this work if he is only a play actor." This pastor was
exactly right. Genuine authenticity and honesty form the bedrock foundations for every phase of ministry.

Credibility Comes from Christ
Degrees, ordination credentials and trappings of ministry, as important as
they seem to us, do not make ministry spiritually authentic. Credibility
comes from Christ alone.

The necessity of our Christ-saturated intimacy shines through these
insightful words from author Richard Lovelace:

> The instruments through which God works in the church are
> human beings, especially pastors. If our hearts and minds are
> not properly transformed, we are like musicians playing
> untuned instruments, or engineers working with broken and
> ill-programmed computers. The attunement of the heart is
> essential to the outflow of grace.[5]

You might want to add an enthusiastic amen while strengthening your
own intimacy with the Savior.

Ministry is more than what we do; its impact depends more on who we are. God wants us to be honest, fair, real—persons of bedrock integrity. These are the only people He uses.

Credibility Enhances Ministry

Believability escalates whenever a pastor lives an exemplary, beautiful Christ-centered life. It becomes a silent, convincing statement made with his life that the pastor is committed to more than minimum requirements of his ordination vows and lives beyond minimal standards of respectable behavior. It is a super vow to God and himself that every expression of ministry will have the highest possible spiritual authenticity and professional quality.

The lovely impact that follows is the exact opposite of what happened when two prominent TV evangelists bit the moral dust. Then everyone—clergy in ministry, individuals on the street and believers in the pew—suffered shock caused by fake charlatans.

Christ-centered living in the pastor helps everyone believe that holy character and integrity are possible and attractive. The power of lived ideals shows in an unsigned letter to the opinion section of the *Denver Post*, "Knowing my priest is holy attracts me to the church and makes me believe I, too, can live a pure life." Credibility counts.

Sterling Behavior Is Rewarded

For a pastor, sterling behavior means more than living up to a worthy, vocational public-image requirement. God plans for Christ-pleasing living to help us enjoy truth, love and wholeness, which is, in itself, a fascinating way to live and provides an enriching energy for meaningful ministry.

Such a lifestyle takes a pastor miles beyond a suffocating code of external conduct into the abounding grandeur of satisfying, noble living. It is written into the moral genetic code of human beings that love feels better than hate, honesty better than chicanery, honor better than corruption and faith better than hopelessness. Expand the list if you wish, but you will discover that godliness always outranks the profane.

Two pastor friends near middle age discussed difficult ethical decisions in their churches. When one expressed hope, despite extreme difficulty, the other joked, "I'm surprised your idealism isn't more corroded after living this long." His comment is more than a joke—corroded ideals have created immense levels of skepticism in some pastors and in even more laypersons.

On the contrary, a minister who lives his ideals while resisting the flood tide of broken promises and flagrant cynicism enjoys sustained satisfactions. He resists the permissiveness he sees in others. He refuses to take moral shortcuts. He allows himself no white lies, no manipulation, no sexual compromise, no financial exploitation and no negotiation of enduring values. He resists shaping his conduct and character by what others do.

A Code of Personal Purity

Here's a code of ideals that fuels sustained satisfaction for a pastor:

"I will be fair, trusting and conscientious in relationships with my family, congregation, community, fellow pastors and community of faith. I will remember who I was when the Lord called me into His sacred service. I will embrace the apostle Paul's specific teaching as my own standard, 'But among you there must not be even a hint of sexual immorality, or of any kind of impurity, or of greed, because these are improper for God's holy people' (Eph. 5:3).

"I will live by the unpretentious standards of Jesus as found in the New Testament. I will live by the letter and the spirit of my marriage and ordination vows. I will obey the law and do good to the best of my ability. I will resist money, sexual and power temptations that come to every pastor. And I will do whatever it takes to make amends should I fail in any of these matters."

How easy to allow one's soul to be shriveled by puny compromises. Although everyone knows about front-page ethical breakdowns, many lesser prominent ministers camouflage dark secrets of their own. They are the walking dead who dread discovery. One pastor expressed regret in retirement years: "If only I had been as good as the people thought I was." Another berated himself: "I sacrificed my influence, my honor and my life's work for 10 minutes of pleasure in a cheap motel room. I feel stupid and dirty."

Self-Evaluation Is Required

Pastors who wish for sustained satisfactions must initiate regular self-evaluation. Like a mountain lookout beside a busy freeway in the Rockies helps one see distant peaks, such self-assessment helps a pastor. It forces a pastor to step out of the day-to-day grind, allows him to see beauty and requires him to be still before God.

Such self-evaluation provides opportunities to ascertain the quality of life—is it lofty and noble, or base and coarse? Such an observation should be inaugurated before moral shipwreck or detrimental circumstances require such stocktaking.

As a starting point, ask yourself the following questions:

- Is my handling of church money squeaky clean?
- Is my use of time ethically authentic?
- Is there disparity between my beliefs and the quality of the sermons I preach and the pastoral care I provide?
- Is my marriage as enjoyable and fulfilling as God intended?
- Do the people I lead believe me to be unequivocally trustworthy?
- Do I deceive myself with self-deception?
- Do my wife and children compete with my ministry?
- Do I accept my part in failures in my life and church?
- Do I flirt with potentially destructive relationships?
- Do I tell half-truths and exaggerate my successes?
- Is my ministry consistent with what I really believe God wants my life to be?

Sustained satisfactions flow from pure living that genuinely pleases God. The mere act of verbalizing and facing these issues can be healing. Above all else, the most magnificent serendipity of such an emancipated life brings sustained satisfaction to a pastor's inner world. He knows God is pleased and he sees his own influence to be convincing and strong and pure. He also knows that he lives a wonderfully fulfilling life—a goal most people search for all their days.

THE PERKS ARE EXTRAORDINARY

What could offer more fulfillment than the satisfactions built into pastoral ministry? I love Gene Fowler's summary, "Love and memory will endure even after the game is called because of darkness."[6] Lasting meaning comes from doing ministry well, as unto Christ and for His glory.

A satisfying memory with its strength and sense of fulfillment may stumble into our minds at any waking moment. Happy recollections of effective service offered in Jesus' name lifts our spirits, especially when our minds begin opening old trunks of pain in the attic of our souls. Try totaling up your exhilarating remembrances. Every pastor has a long list of sustained satisfactions—many he tends to forget or downplay.

Where else could such authentic meaning be found? Who else enjoys such unique fulfillment in their work? How else could I find such sustained satisfaction down to the last day of old age and into heaven? There also are many abounding personal perks that flow from the people of God to make me rich.

With astounding indebtedness, I relive priceless experiences when ministry became a boomerang given back to me by the ones I served.

From parishioners I learned new ways to trust my weary soul to the grace of God as I saw people in the congregations live faith in the midst of overwhelming calamities.

When my failures embarrassed or humiliated me, I cherished loving words I received from the people of God who believed in me.

When my family was up against it in medical crises and tough financial times, I remember kindness and generosity from many who stood by us in our time of need.

You can tell how much gratitude I feel for those who bore burdens with me in long-ago pastorates. I rejoice over victories we celebrated together. Although many people might believe I have forgotten their kindnesses over these long years, much of it is as fresh as this morning's dawn.

One theological educator and mentor offered this counsel to a greenhorn pastor: "With good memories of deeds done and kindness received, a pastor is safe in the thick and thin of ministry. He can rise to any challenge and face anything as a consequence of those two memories."

ENJOY THE PERKS TO THE MAXIMUM

Opportunities of sustained satisfactions surround every servant of Christ. Rejoice in the extraordinary benefits God has planted in your ministry, both on Main Street and in the out-of-the-way back corners of pastoral routine. Maximize your unique perks. Cherish the adventures that flow from a Christ-saturated ministry.

Many pastoral perks are paid immediately. Others are paid in installments for a lifetime. Some sneak up on us from ministry given half a lifetime ago. And the most significant payoff is yet to come when the Father says, "Well done!"

Savor the sustained satisfactions that surround you. Allow them to cultivate an exciting marriage, to rear outstanding children and to build a supernatural church in a place where they said it couldn't be done. More than anything else, allow ministry to help you grow a life that is honorable and authentic and free from imprisonments that conniving and control always cause.

CONTEMPORARY CHALLENGE
YOUR PERKS MAKE YOU SPIRITUALLY RICH

- You represent Christ at life's main events.
- You enjoy a front-row seat at grace happenings.
- You have a partnership with omnipotence.
- Your congregation loves you.

- Your marriage and ministry can nourish each other.
- Your church wants to affirm your children.
- Your spiritual development is a serendipity of effective ministry.
- Your home can be an emotional sanctuary.
- Your ministry allows you to turn vision into achievements.
- Your specialty helps people cope with life.

Every person carries in his heart a blueprint of the One he loves. — Fulton Sheen[7]

Notes
1. C. S. Lewis, "The Weight of Glory," as quoted in *Christianity Today*, Vol. 37, No. 6, May 17, 1993, p. 40.
2. *St. Louis Post-Dispatch*, May 1, 1993, 4B.
3. George Barna, *Today's Pastors* (Ventura, CA: Regal Books, 1993), p. 33.
4. Paul Pearsall, *Power of the Family* (New York: Bantam Books, 1991), p. 4.
5. Richard Lovelace, *Dynamics of Spiritual Life* (Downers Grove, IL: InterVarsity Press, 1979), p. 16.
6. James B. Simpson, Compiler, *Simpson's Contemporary Quotations* (Boston, MA: Houghton Mifflin Co., 1988), p. 227.
7. Fulton Sheen, *On Being Human* (Garden City, NY: Image Books, 1983), p. 211.

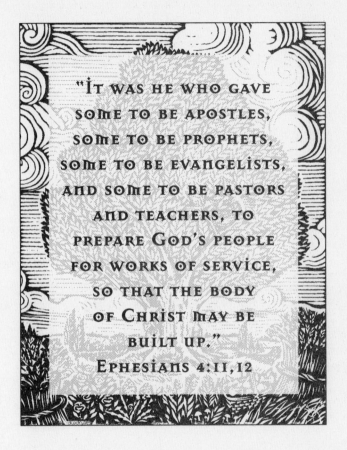

"It was he who gave some to be apostles, some to be prophets, some to be evangelists, and some to be pastors and teachers, to prepare God's people for works of service, so that the body of Christ may be built up."

Ephesians 4:11,12

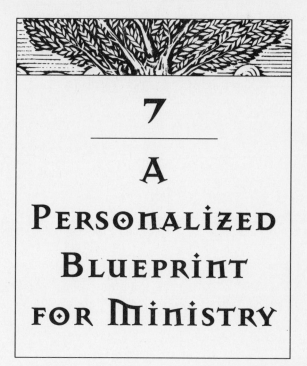

7

A PERSONALIZED BLUEPRINT FOR MINISTRY

Holy Father, make me faithful to Kingdom priorities.
Use my gifts for your glory, my abilities for your people,
my strength for your service.
Amen.

YOU ARE UNIQUELY GIFTED FOR A DISTINCTIVE MINISTRY

God loves variety. He designed infinite diversity into the Creation. In nature, His originality shows in every maple leaf, every snowflake and every mountain peak. His humorous originality even shows in human noses, voices and toes.

God made you unique and different from every other human being. This fact shows in your deoxyribonucleic acid (DNA) profile, which looks like an expanded bar code that supermarkets use to check prices. It is, however, more than a price code. It is a detailed blueprint that answers questions about you, ranging from color of hair to parentage to potential to length of life.

Scientific researchers say your DNA makes you different from every other human being. Your DNA is as singular as your signature and can be used to establish your identity with more reliability than conventional blood-typing that is used to implicate suspects in criminal cases. In fact, geneticists can pinpoint more than 4,000 hereditary diseases from the study of DNA.[1]

God created you as a unique person so He could use you in a special way. Therefore, the Creator does not want you to imitate someone else. He does, however, want you to yield to His will and purpose so He can help you accomplish something important for the kingdom of God.

A TV commercial tells the story well. Four children are asked in the commercial what they want to be when they grow up. One said, "I want to be a fireman." Another, "I want to be a doctor." The third, "I want to be a basketball star." But the fourth said it the biblical way, "I want to be myself."

Every pastor needs to grasp the insight behind that last remark. He must cherish his uniqueness and not try to copy anyone else. Neither should anyone expect him to be like another, especially a pastor before him.

Frustrated by Unmet Aspirations

An urban pastor whom I (H. B.) know feels locked into his suburban pastorate. It's a good place, but he doesn't feel like he fits it anymore. It is a setting many of his colleagues would love. He is in midlife and feels he will never fulfill his dream of being a maverick pastor in an inner city.

In a letter he wrote to me about his frustrations, he said, "I have always wanted to work in the inner city. I dream of supporting myself with a secular job and serving as a bivocational pastor among poor people. The concept I wanted to try was to be a worker-pastor, different from any traditional ministries I have ever seen.

"I don't know if it would work, but the suburbs bore me more every day. Must of the time I feel like I am baby-sitting immature Christians; their money and tradition seem to make the problem bigger than it really is. The spark is gone. Now life is passing too quickly; I doubt I will ever get to try my idea."

How sad that what he desires most eludes him at a time he is needed in the cities. How sad, too, for those pastors who would like to have what he has. He would gladly move to the city if he could figure out ways to get started and to raise the money.

The lesson for all: Turning one's back on curiosities and aspirations decimates satisfaction, causes long-term feelings of defeat and undermines the effectiveness of our current ministry.

Trapped by Boring Assignments

Surveys show that many pastors feel locked into their assignments. Perhaps they belong to a denominational system such as the Methodist governmental structure that sometimes places pastors in situations and locations they might not desire. Other pastors have been in an assignment for many years where the congregation or the neighborhood has changed, but the ministries have remained unchanged.

Other pastors serve traditional churches that have remained unchanged while they themselves have grown or have changed perspectives. Still others want to move to a smaller church after their church has grown beyond their ability to cope. Some preretirement pastors wish to slow down while their churches want to be more progressive and to sponsor more activities.

Location frustration, whatever the cause, should be admitted and solved in one of two ways. If a pastor cannot change his sense of being trapped, for personal well-being and wholeness, he should seek to move to another assignment or to start a new ministry.

Another option is available, one that is at the heart of this book. Try staying where you are and making the place holy ground. Most of the time, location frustration is a problem in the pastor's psyche and is not well known or even considered important by members of the congregation.

The solution for location frustration starts by developing a specific blueprint of ministry for your present setting that makes room for two things: the most pressing needs of the setting and the maximum use of your personal talents and abilities.

√Cultivate Your Uniqueness

When God created you, He made a blueprint of a distinctive ministry for you. He designed you to do something special for Him, something no one else does as well as you can. He likely wants it done where you now serve. Cloning is not the way God works in your ministry or in anyone else's. No other person is capable or talented to accomplish what God has mapped out for you.

God believes so much in your gifts and devotion that He chooses a risky strategy for changing His world through people like you. God allows you immense freedom to discover what ministry is suitable for you and how you will use the gifts He has given you. He even allows autonomy about where ministry is done.

This freedom creates confusion for the Kingdom and for us when it is misused. It tends to complicate the church's placement procedures for pastors. To bewilder matters more, we are often overly modest or shy about telling others what we know we can do best. We reason it could sound like self-promotion or could appear that we covet a particular assignment. Then, again, we might not know what we do well, so we have nothing to tell anyone else.

Ministerial tedium multiples when a pastor buries his talents. Maximum fulfillment develops, however, from being at the right place at the right time with the right skills to accomplish a magnificent work for Christ. When a pastor fails to use his unique giftedness, the Kingdom and his specific congregation suffer. As a result, his disillusionment increases, his impact declines and he denies a congregation the talents God intended to be used in his ministry.

Excellence Brings Satisfaction

God wants magnificent competence in every aspect of ministry. A personal commitment to competence determines the difference between

excellence and mediocrity. God detests shoddy work and is always a little embarrassed when someone announces, "I want to be faithful even if
I can't do ministry very well."

Why not do both? Why not give God a combination of competence
and faithfulness? The Father multiplies satisfaction for those who do their
work well. Competence is a habit and so is shoddiness. Doing ministry
well produces incredible impact for the cause of Christ even as it brings
indescribable exhilaration.

We Need a Divine Helping Hand

Playing the pastoral perfection game usually leads to a miserably shallow
ministry. No pastor even comes close to being perfect in his performance
of ministry. Although we might hate to admit it, most of us easily identify with a pastor who snorted, "I specialize in fallibility." The apostle
Paul candidly rejoiced in the fact that ministry was essentially impossible
for him without divine enablement. And the same is true for us.

The other day, a district superintendent asked me to read a statement
he wrote to lay leaders of a church in crises. In essence, his excellent
statement said, "I feel inadequate to help you, but I never want to be
involved in any facet of ministry that I could not do without God's help."
His message was crystal clear: I want to help, but I need supernatural
assistance to do very much. His message sounds a lot like Jesus' word that
we must be connected to the vine if our ministry is to produce anything
worthwhile.

Although rarely discussed, this issue of presumed competence may be
among the most compelling problems in the contemporary church. No
matter how favorably educated or fervently zealous, no one is qualified
enough, insightful enough or talented enough to do effective ministry
without the energizing enablement of the Omnipotent One.

Sadly, too much ministry is attempted in human strength alone and it
goes nowhere. But supernatural resources are promised to those who seek
and use them. God chooses to use people who depend on Him.

Team Effort Pays Dividends

Dependency on members of the congregation is also important.

Admitting need and asking for help is not easy in our "can-do" world. In the Church, however, such an admission often begins a lovely experience of shared service in Jesus' name. Strange as it seems, the people of God are quick to offer acceptance and to assist when a pastor admits frailties and needs.

People naturally step forward to help a pastor who acknowledges inadequacies. Such self-revelation somehow motivates people to help. The results are wonderful: The helpers find satisfaction, the cause is advanced and a pastor feels encouraged by the team effort.

Pastor Was Too Flawless
The all-too-common perfection game shackles a pastor with self-imposed paralyzing demands. In such circumstances, a pastor feels forced to act as if he knows everything or pretends to be more pious than he is.

One beginning pastor found out the hard way. He was young and handsome in a rugged kind of way. He had an excellent education and enjoyed a storybook marriage. With many impressive personal and professional assets, he started his first pastorate overloaded with confidence and expecting perfection from everyone, including himself.

Although his pastorate was a near disaster from the start, he kept trying harder and harder. When he faced demands where he had no experience or training, he bluffed his way to make a good impression. Each time he encountered these kind of situations, his self-confidence eroded a little more and his satisfactions dissipated.

He soon learned an excruciating lesson: No one can do ministry perfectly all the time. Much to his surprise, when the crunch came and he admitted it, his congregation overlooked his inadequacies with a shrug. More than one volunteer said, "We're relieved to see you are not perfect. We like preachers who are human like us." To relish sustained satisfaction, a minister must come to terms with his lack of experience, his weaknesses and his toxic need to be perfect.

Perfection Fuels Fantasies
Perfection sometimes shows up in other ways, too. For some pastors, by the time they come to midlife or before, self-justification or denials have

accumulated into mind-breaking loads. They cannot be perfect, but they pretend to be.

A weary minister is then no longer able to accurately evaluate his work and his ideas. So without intending to do so, he creates a fantasy of who he is, what his church can be and how important he is to the congregation.

As a result, he takes up permanent residency in his mind on Main Street in Make Believe, USA. Recently, I met a 69-year-old pastor who has lived at such a phony address for more than 30 years.

Ministers of this kind have a frame of reference that resembles a medieval castle surrounded by a deep moat of water filled with angry alligators. Sadly, no drawbridge spans the moat to help pastors move into the real world or for others to rescue them. They live in a make-believe world, believing their contribution in ministry is greater than it really is. The pastor perfection game makes them that way.

Beware of Becoming a Fish Keeper

One pastor I know also lives by fantasies that are influenced by a need to be perfect. Although his congregation tolerates him like a friendly, aging great-uncle, he seems out of touch, unaware of the pivotal issues of contemporary Christianity and takes comfort in being a keeper of a placid tiny aquarium. He seems satisfied to feed a few fish a monotonous diet every Sunday at 11:00 A.M. and to scour the fish tank now and then.

Sadly, he completely missed the excitement of ever doing ministry exceptionally well. Because of his perspective, people he touches with his ministry consider Christianity too dull for a thinking person to consider.

Pathetically, many pastors who are infected with this chronic disease know something is cockeyed. Because they do not know what to do, they do nothing. For them, it just seems easier to brush off bad news than to deal with it. One overstressed leader remarked, "I don't know who the enemy is." The enemy was likely inside him and he didn't realize it.

Work Increases, Results Decline

My first conversation with a pastor I'll call Vince Delong, dealt with his confusion about ministry. Delong, a 15-year veteran of a 125-member church, asked me to be a sounding board as he thought out loud about his future. He felt unnerved and afraid as he explained, "I try harder and get fewer results now than at any time in my ministry. I keep working longer hours, but I get less and less response."

Thinking a few new members might fix his problems, Pastor Delong drove himself untiringly. He kept busy so he could dodge tension his church problems caused at home. Draining bustle replaced meaning for him. He was tired and depressed.

As I listened, he moved deeper into his disappointments: "Six wonderful couples in their middle 30s moved out of our congregation to other area churches in the last four months. They represent the spiritual backbone and economic core of this congregation.

"The loss is simply staggering. The last couple blasted me with these words just before they left, 'You don't get it, do you? We all joined this church because of you, but you have changed, and not for the better. You used to keep up with the times, but you now operate the church in a tired old way like you did 10 years ago. It just won't cut it anymore.' I worry that they may be right."

Vince's problems, like many contemporary pastors, are not doctrinal or moral but relate to outlook and methods. Although those members who deserted probably could not describe it, they sensed in him a great unwillingness—almost naïveté—to face the real world.

It appeared to them to be an unhealthy fixation on the past, which made them lose interest. They left because they saw no possibility for improvement. What a sad predicament for everyone—for those who left, for those who stayed and especially for the pastor.

For the purpose of our discussion, it is necessary to deal only with the pastor and not with the laity. For Vince to enjoy spiritual and emotional wellness, he must be willing to recognize and to correct several weaknesses.

It is not being perfect but striving for competence. Pastor-writer Robert Hudnut's comment speaks precisely to this problem: "Rather than being paralyzed by his faults, a pastor must acknowledge them and push ahead in spite of them. Fortunately, the job makes the person in the ministry even more than the person makes the job. Weaknesses can be forged into strengths. But facing and correcting weaknesses helps keep ministers effective."[2]

Facing Frailties Blunts Egotism

This tricky task of identifying and correcting weaknesses pays off with self-understanding and professional growth. Such an effort blasts an inflated ego and helps a pastor see ministry through the eyes of those who live life at the front lines of contemporary life.

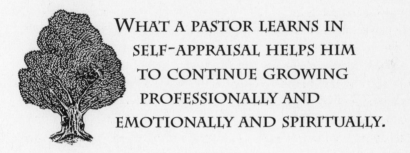

WHAT A PASTOR LEARNS IN SELF-APPRAISAL HELPS HIM TO CONTINUE GROWING PROFESSIONALLY AND EMOTIONALLY AND SPIRITUALLY.

Without such self-understanding, it is incredibly easy for an ego-driven pastor to form obnoxious attitudes and to demonstrate self-centered behavior. Then he berates inflexibility, manipulation, compulsiveness or suspicious ethics in others without recognizing those faults in himself.

Conversely, enduring fulfillments often grow out of an accurate assessment of a pastor's work and an awareness of personal identity. What a pastor learns in self-appraisal helps him to continue growing professionally and emotionally and spiritually. Sustained satisfactions usually follow.

MAINTAIN A HANDS-ON MINISTRY

Efficient delegation is an important element of contemporary ministry, and hands-on ministry is decreasing. Without question, a congregation is healthier spiritually when a pastor shares ministry with church members.

This useful trend means that empowering the laity increases their spiritual development and more work gets done.

Such a partnership in ministry is necessary for efficiency and for increased fulfillment of laity. Consider the examples. Pastoral care is now being shared and many lay leaders are doing this phase of ministry well and with satisfaction. Administrative functions are increasingly being assigned to laypersons, and they are doing them well. Bible teaching has been shared for centuries. Shouldering such responsibilities encourages an overdue renewal of the laity and gives them meaning once reserved only for the clergy. All of this is positive and useful—more of it is needed.

However, all ministry cannot be delegated to others. No pastor can fully bloom and grow when he only manages and assigns ministry to others. He, himself, must take the towel and the basin. He must rejoice with young families at the birth of their children, and he must weep with the dying. He does not need to do all the ministry, nor can he, but he must do some of it.

A pastor forfeits a keen ingredient of ministry when he no longer ministers to others on a regular basis. He gives up a spiritually satisfying bond between pastor and parishioner that is not available in any other way. This essential connection is among the most satisfying motivations for being a pastor; to give it up completely is to give up something precious and needed for personal fulfillment.

Such commitment to a pastor's personal involvement does not deny service opportunities to others. It simply means the minister must keep in touch or he will be unfulfilled and out of sync. The paradox is to continue personal ministry while giving much of it away. Participation and delegation are needed in contemporary pastoral work. No minister can continue to bloom who isolates himself from the sinful, hurting and dying.

Don't Take Authority Too Seriously

Authority and influence do not make you special or different from other people. Such privilege simply places greater demands on the trusted leader. A pastor needs to remind himself often that ordination or installation in a church as pastor does not make him infallible.

Simply holding ecclesiastical, organizational or ordination authority does not mean a pastor knows how to make flawless decisions automatically. It does not mean he can think better than anyone else. Nor does it mean he is more spiritual than members of the group.

Admittedly, the person holding the highest position in church structures usually gets his way, regardless of who is right. Pastors sometimes resent this reality in relationships to their ecclesiastical superiors. What happens in the upward organizational flow in churches also happens in a downward flow in local congregations.

As a result, pastors sometimes misuse authority. This means that a pastor who wants to be effective in a spiritual sense must sometimes willingly lose an administrative decision because his judgment is in error. Authority in itself never makes a leader unerring.

Use of authority is complicated even more when lay members of a church's decision group comply with their pastor's wishes simply because they want to be cooperative. Because complying is not commitment, organizational and relational disasters sometimes follow.

A pastor who insists on having his own way will then find himself followed by a group who submit to his domination but do not accept his leadership. He may hold a rope in his hand but it is not attached to anything that matters. Such bullheaded use of authority causes spiritual and organizational stagnation.

On the contrary, a spiritually aware leader will work for consensus, ownership and refinement of ideas. His ministry then blooms because he uses the best judgment he receives from advisers. He builds strong morale in the process. Our Lord empowered others for greatness by loving them, trusting them and holding them spiritually accountable. His pattern helps us bloom, too.

Commit to Lifelong Development

Effective pastors learn from every possible source all the days of their lives. An example that comes to mind is a man in his late 30s who entered the ministry as a self-made country preacher. He brought exceptional people skills to ministry that had been developed when he was a small-business owner. But formal learning and ministerial development continued low on his priority list. He reasoned, "I already know how to get along with people."

Soon after launching his ministry, he realized he had to study to keep up with the demands. Surprising to him, something amazing happened. He started seeing the world as a wonderful learning place where people, events and situations taught him a great deal he could use in ministry. Now he says, "I love to learn and I hope it shows." It does.

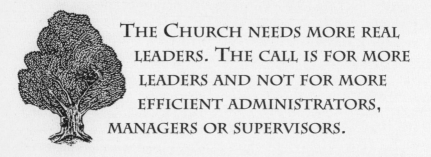

THE CHURCH NEEDS MORE REAL LEADERS. THE CALL IS FOR MORE LEADERS AND NOT FOR MORE EFFICIENT ADMINISTRATORS, MANAGERS OR SUPERVISORS.

Many pastors are personally and professionally plateaued because they seldom consider a fresh thought. Others shut their minds the day they receive their diploma or degree. How sad to miss so much. Learning and personal development can be fun and always help a pastor bloom where he is planted.

Pay the Price to Lead
The church needs more real leaders. Recently, researcher George Barna wrote in his book *Today's Pastors*:

> During a decade of study, I have become increasingly convinced that the Church struggles not because it lacks enough zealots who will join the crusade for Christ, not because it lacks the tangible resources to do the job and not because it has withered into a muddled understanding of its fundamental beliefs. The problem is the Christian church is not led by true leaders.[3]

What a stunning indictment and what a frightening appraisal! Apparently, administration, management and supervision are done reasonably well in many churches. But the call is for more leaders and not for more efficient administrators, managers or supervisors.

Leadership, for our purposes, might be defined as a pastor who generates positive spiritual achievement in a congregation. A genuine pastor-leader sees his task as much more than being a resident saint, showing up for church, preserving the establishment and spending the money.

In his book *Developing the Leader Within You*, Pastor John C. Maxwell describes a congregation that is led by a genuine pastor-leader: "Morale is high. Turnover is low. Needs are being met. Goals are being realized....Leading and influencing others is fun. Problems are solved with minimum effort. Fresh statistics are shared on a regular basis with the people that undergird the growth of the organization."[4]

The Church of Jesus Christ at every level of her life and ministry needs leaders who are able to establish and to communicate vision.

Let's realize that not all authentic leadership starts with being given an important post, although much of it does. Neither does genuine leadership automatically come with an appointment—a person can hold a pastoral position for a lifetime without being a leader.

Conversely, designated official leaders do not always exert the greatest influence in a church or organization. Tillich, Huxley and Oates—a strange trio—all speak with approval about a type of leader who lives at the periphery of an organization or congregation. A short sentence from Huxley explains, "It is not at the center, not from within the organization, that the saint can cure our regimented insanity; it is only from without, at the periphery."[5]

The peripheral leader's tools are friendly persuasion, unquestioned love and loyalty for the cause of Christ. In times of confusion or crises, the peripheral leader may be heeded for the strength of his ideas alone. Perhaps the Church needs an army of peripheral leaders for times likes these.

From firsthand observation and personal correspondence, compelling evidence shows that many pastors are not equipped or educated or experienced for the job typical churches need them to do. Neither are they able to lead effective outreach in the contemporary world.

Barna believes this leadership shortage revolves around the Church's

ability to identify potential leaders, the way pastors are typically prepared, the way ministers are evaluated and the way clergy are supported.[6]

Barna's chapter in *Today's Pastors* on "Training Leaders to Lead" and
numerous other books and magazine articles suggest massive reforms are
needed in ministerial preparation. Barna may be right. Something much
more immediate is needed, however, because if his proposed changes
were started at once in Bible colleges and seminaries, they would have little effect on people now active in ministry.

Consequently, pastors must strengthen their leadership skills in every
imaginable way. Books, seminars and mentoring will help. But a closer,
more convenient learning resource is often overlooked. Many never
think to view the Church and the world as living classrooms.

To increase leadership competence, a pastor must keep alert to life.
Such development demands that he listen carefully for leadership lessons
from common people as well as from professionals. It means applying
ideas from every source to the ministry. It quizzes trend-setting ministers.
It observes and questions pacesetters in business and government. In fact,
a developing leader will be open to insights and ideas from every source.

An achievement-driven leader takes what he learns from life and
applies the data to ministry. An imaginative pastor-leader schools himself
to consider how a concept, program or principle can improve his ministry.

Such a continual state of "how can I make it better" helps formulate a
church's future. Such filtering of the environment helps a leader success-
fully ride the frightening waves of the future to new ways of thinking and
doing.

Dedication to betterment of personal leadership keeps a pastor
blooming anywhere, even in the winters of ministry. It prevents a pastor
from becoming out of date. Such persistent individual development
encourages laypersons to use their childlike curiosity in Kingdom adventures.

Beyond our managing, influencing, directing, preaching, administer-
ing and teaching, a growing pastor-leader challenges people to hope,
love, believe, compassion, wonder, reverence and grace.

By reaching deep into these never-dry, ever-fresh springs, we equip fellow pilgrims to be dreamers of dreams, to be passionate risk takers who transform churches and communities and to create Christ-alive churches.

All of these resources will produce stunningly beautiful blooms in any ecclesiastical leadership garden.

CONTEMPORARY CHALLENGE
FOLLOW GOD'S BLUEPRINT

- God loves diversity.
- God created you unique.
- God expects competence.
- God empowers our best efforts.
- God resources growth.

The block of granite which was an obstacle in the pathway of the weak becomes a stepping stone in the pathway of the strong. — Thomas Carlyle[7]

Notes
1. *Colorado Springs Gazette Telegraph*, Feb. 21, 1994, 1A; *U.S. News and World Report*, Jan 27, 1992; *National Geographic*, May 1992, page 112.
2. Robert K. Hudnut, *Surprised by God* (New York: The Associated Press, 1967), p. 125.

3. George Barna, *Today's Pastors* (Ventura, CA: Regal Books, 1993), p. 137.
4. John C. Maxwell, *Developing the Leader Within You* (Nashville: Thomas Nelson Publishers, 1993), p. 9.
5. As quoted in Wayne Oates' *Ape and Essence* (New York: HarperCollins, 1948), p. 6.
6. Barna, *Today's Pastors*, p. 137.
7. As quoted by Ted Engstrom, *The Making of a Christian Leader* (Grand Rapids, MI: Zondervan Publishing House, 1976), p. 85.

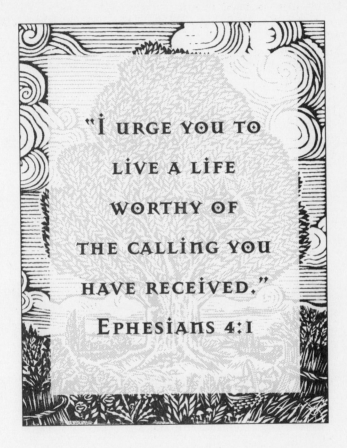

"I URGE YOU TO LIVE A LIFE WORTHY OF THE CALLING YOU HAVE RECEIVED."

EPHESIANS 4:1

8

GROW
A GREAT
SOUL

*Father, walk with me in my pilgrimage as a pastor to
mountain peaks that I may see Your purposes clearly,
lush pastures that I may be nourished by Your truth,
valleys of discouragement that I may be supported by Your
strength. May Your gentleness make me great.
Amen.*

GETTING INTO SHAPE SPIRITUALLY

"You know that God took a rib out of man to create woman," a minister
joked while introducing a Bible study during a men's fellowship. "The rib
was taken out of the wrong place, however," the speaker declared, smil-
ing and motioning to his expanding waist. Without intending to do so,
he called attention to his obesity.

Pastors, like everyone else, are concerned about being in good shape
physically. Early on, they watch their diets and burn off calories through

a variety of physical activities. They soon learn, however, that without a dogged discipline they often fall victim to the tyranny of the urgent, to overcrowded schedules, to too many meat-potato-and-gravy meals, to expanding belts and to drooping stomachs.

It is easy for pastors to become out of shape spiritually, too. They have expended their spiritual stamina in long hours of preaching, teaching and counseling and have little reserve available to keep their souls in shape.

We know that if we try to function without spiritual energy, we feel perpetually spent and stressed. We fret over the discrepancies between what is and what ought to be. Then the momentum of ministry makes us dizzy, and we grow bone weary. Without ever getting fired up, we burn out. Sometimes we even feel forced to fake piety because it is expected—what John Henry Jowett calls "being professors but not pilgrims."[1] Ministry then becomes a mere responsibility to fulfill or a frustrating job that can easily be cast off when the going gets tough.

When the flame of devotion burns low, a pastor's performance sinks to a shocking state. Every task requires too much effort. An accumulation of weariness corrodes a minister's soul, sabotages his ministry and shatters his concept of self. Ministry then dies a slow, miserable death and is buried under a tombstone marked: "No vision because I forgot Jesus could help me."

A spiritual shallowness then colors every aspect of life. The pastor feels disheartened and is easily tempted. A warning comes from Alexander Solzhenitsyn: "The meaning of earthly existence lies not, as we have grown used to thinking, in prospering but in the development of the soul."[2]

We know and preach that spiritual conditioning produces the best quality of life. But for some strange reason, pastors frequently compartmentalize professional ministry and personal faith so that the two cannot draw on each other. In such situations, the minister soon starts functioning like a religious robot, rather than as a caring pastor. Soon he is rootless, overextended, reactionary and scared.

Growing a great soul promises so much more. It helps us remember that God intends every aspect of life and ministry to be intricately woven around Christ. This focus is for our own development as much as it is for vibrant ministry. To grow a beautiful life, the Father gives us forgiveness, grace, hope, love and faith. He wants life and ministry to be tied together with meaning, value and beauty.

RAW MATERIALS ARE EVERYWHERE

During a grueling church construction program, the kind that often makes great demands upon a pastor, I (Neil) struggled to finish my Christmas sermon. In an effort to clear my mental cobwebs, I took a walk along the Atlantic Ocean a few blocks from my church. For most of the morning, my sermonic wrestling had been dealing largely with the conceptual aspects of the Incarnation accounts in Scripture.

Something supernatural occurred that morning. As I walked by the sea, all nature seemed to be singing the songs of Christmas. As I admired the moving tide and tried to take in the full range of colors of sky and sea, an "aha" moment splashed at my feet and changed ministry forever for me.

At that moment, I experienced the birth of Christ in a profoundly personal way. Incarnation power was no longer a novel and seasonal Scripture to be preached every Advent. On that day, the Incarnation became an intimate treasure, something to share. Ministry began enriching me and feeding my soul in many new ways. My ministry still serves other people as it always has, but it also feeds my personal inwardness. Ministry develops me even as I offer it to others. That satisfying two-way process continues today. I am a better Christian because of the demands of ministry.

Think of the possibilities for all of us in the recognition of this reality. Ministry takes me to the heart of the richest of all resources for anyone's personal growth. Therefore, to preach is to deal with raw materials of faith; so when I preach great truths of Scripture, I am molded by them even as God uses the same passages to shape others through me.

Pastoral care gives us a beautiful window of opportunity to apply faith to the happiest and to the saddest episodes of human life. Administrative tasks and leadership responsibilities allow me to put faith into practice.

Therefore, to do ministry means I am dealing with spiritual resources that make my soul strong and my faith muscular.

All of this is an amazing, though seldom recognized, reality of ministry. While I work to save souls and to develop disciples, I grow into the image of Christlikeness. Like a gourmet cook preparing a meal, I enjoy incredible opportunities to taste scrumptious food and to fatten my soul.

Maximize the Opportunities for Spiritual Fitness
To ripen his soul, a pastor must build a basic presupposition into his practice of ministry. To cultivate a sturdy soul, he must view ministry as a colossal opportunity for personal spiritual development. Although he is obviously called to serve God and a congregation, he is surrounded by raw materials to nurture his own growth.

As a beginning point, a pastor must view spiritual growth as much more than religious veneer for public display. Rather, spirituality must be valued as an essential ingredient for growing a satisfying life that begins at our innermost center and connects with the most minute details of human experience. The resulting captivating possibilities energize life and ministry.

To keep spiritually fit, we must recognize that spiritual maturity does not come by a natural or automatic osmosis. Handling holy things and communicating profound biblical ideas never make us holy. Leading religious events and competent preaching do not make us godly. Neither is spiritual development caught like a flu virus from a mate, a mentor or a church member.

Regrettably, some pastors settle for spiritual shallowness although they are surrounded by gold mines of raw materials. It is easy for them to become overly familiar with God's sublime provisions.

Use Spiritual Dynamite
Check the facts and reevaluate the opportunities. Pastors are continually exposed to spiritual-development opportunities in their day-by-day ministry. Even the busiest pastor holds spiritual dynamite in his hands many hours every day.

Teaching and preaching take the minister to the Book of God—the oxygen line of spiritual health. Ministers pray public and private prayers often and everywhere, and they often see supernatural results. Counseling and pastoral care take them to the middle of spiritual action where they see lives changed, marriages healed and spirits reformed. The challenge is to make fuller use of these close-at-hand opportunities to draw our souls closer to God.

Make Ministry More than a Profession

For years, society viewed pastors as bumbling but harmless people. Everyone was expected to respect them, but not everyone took them seriously. Although this attitude still prevails in some places, it has radically changed in others.

Now, pastors are often well trained, skilled in their work and professionally credentialed. Now, citywide ministerial associations sometimes

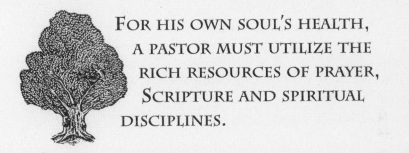

FOR HIS OWN SOUL'S HEALTH, A PASTOR MUST UTILIZE THE RICH RESOURCES OF PRAYER, SCRIPTURE AND SPIRITUAL DISCIPLINES.

look much like a professional meeting of doctors or lawyers. In such an environment, it is easy for a pastor to allow ministry to become overly professionalized and spiritually undernourished.

A balance is needed between call and competency, professionalism and character. No one need criticize or fret about a professional focus if improved skill, training, understanding and approval of his peers is what is intended. Even the most highly trained, sophisticated pastor must remain close to the basics of faith and to the foundation that God has set him apart for a lofty, holy task—a partnership with Him. For his soul's health, a minister must utilize the rich resources of prayer, Scripture and spiritual disciplines. He must keep his faith warm and assuring. He must love righteousness and show mercy.

We give up too much if we lose the heart and soul out of ministry by overly professionalizing it. The desired objective is to conduct ourselves like competent professionals and to trust God like dependent servants.

Follow a Strict Spiritual Fitness Regimen

Try to view growing a great soul through a medical lens: A license to practice medicine, a thorough knowledge of pharmacology and 30 years' surgical experience do not keep a physician personally well. He may practice medicine without being healthy himself. But a healthy medical doctor must apply the same rules of good health for himself as he gives his patients, or he will be as sick as they are.

One undebatable axiom for ministry must be faced. Personal spiritual growth is absolutely essential for a pastor if he wants to enjoy sustained satisfactions and beneficial ministry. A pastor must take his spiritual fitness seriously just as a physician must give attention to his own physical health. He must apply to himself the remedies and suggestions he prescribes for others.

Retain Freshness

A pastor's spiritual fitness requires fresh encounters with God in traditional, faith-formation exercises of prayer, Scripture reading, fasting, devotional reading, soul friendships and centering on Christ. Freshness may be more important than frequency.

Eugene H. Peterson, a long-time pastor and an insightful eyewitness of present-day ministry, shares this perceptive observation: "Three pastoral acts—praying, reading Scripture and giving spiritual direction—are so basic, so critical, that they determine the shape of everything else in ministry. Besides being basic, these three acts are quiet and done mostly out of the spotlight of public ministry. Because they do not call attention to themselves, they are so often neglected....Because almost never does anyone notice whether we do these things or not, and only occasionally does someone ask that we do them, these real acts of ministry suffer widespread neglect."[3] When any of these pastoral acts is neglected, the minister and his congregation are seriously shortchanged.

Peterson amplifies his warning: "It doesn't take many years in the pastorate to realize that we can conduct a fairly respectable ministry without giving much more than ceremonial attention to God. Because we can omit these acts without anybody noticing, and because each of the acts involves a great deal of rigor, it is easy and common to slight them."[4] Vitality leaks out of ministry when a pastor makes his own spirituality ceremonial and perfunctory.

The task is to infuse spirituality with soul, spirit and expectation. The routines must be fueled by creativity, imagination, spontaneity, delight or even fascination. Consequently, spiritual wellness takes more than praying louder or longer. It also requires more than reading an additional 50 Bible verses each day. The point is to find personal spiritual nourishment in every expression of devotion.

This relationship is like family bonding that draws one close to the Father. Longing and originality and intention then become fully as important as sentiment or length or sameness. Cultivating an adventuresome closeness to God is the overriding goal. Without it, vigor and stamina burn low or go out.

Cultivate a God-Permeated Life

A pastor who served a congregation of about 100 for more than two decades calls this close, Christ connection "a God-permeated life." What a word picture. The components consist of devotion to Scripture, intimacy in prayer and friendship with saints who walk across the pages of devotional literature. It also esteems contemporary, ordinary persons who do heroic service for God in out-of-the-way churches or in unheralded settings.

Our effort to grow a great soul means we allow the discoveries of past pilgrims to shape us until the stories of biblical characters and devotional saints become our own. Their quest, then, becomes ours, so we grow like they grew, we bloom like they bloomed and we produce fruits of righteousness like they did. And we live what they lived—at home, in the church and everywhere.

Thus, spiritual formation means getting together often with God. To use teenage language, we hang out with Him. This God-closeness, like falling in love, creates attentiveness, togetherness and warmth. This deepening intimacy with God opens our eyes to see amazing mysteries of grace and provides fulfillment throughout a lifetime of ministry.

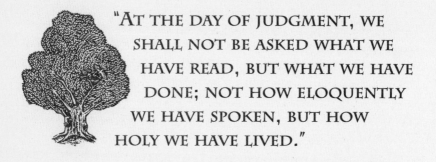

"AT THE DAY OF JUDGMENT, WE SHALL NOT BE ASKED WHAT WE HAVE READ, BUT WHAT WE HAVE DONE; NOT HOW ELOQUENTLY WE HAVE SPOKEN, BUT HOW HOLY WE HAVE LIVED."

Such Christ-closeness is more than a private adventure for a pastor. It is like an electrical conduit through which divine enablement flows through us into our ministry. Pastors experience such empowerment as they welcome the One T. S. Eliot described in his prayer:

Oh, my soul, be prepared for the coming of the Stranger,
Be prepared for Him who knows how to ask questions.[5]

CHRIST—THE SOURCE FOR LIFELONG SPIRITUAL GROWTH

How, then, is a great soul grown? Authentic ministry fitness comes from standing at full attention before the Chief—Peter Marshall's splendid phrase—and doing what our Commander orders.

The urgency for personal spiritual development is emphasized in Thomas Kempis's warning, "At the day of judgment, we shall not be asked what we have read, but what we have done; not how eloquently we have spoken, but how holy we have lived."[6]

This endeavor to grow his soul energizes commitment in churches, inspires Christlikeness in laity and generates incredible satisfaction for a pastor. Every effort to keep spiritually fit activates Christ's extravagant promise, "Blessed are those who hunger and thirst for righteousness, *for they will be filled*" (Matt. 5:6, italics added).

Personal Spiritual Growth Illuminates Vision

Ministry seems fuzzy. By this, we mean that current pastoral effort often appears to be fixed on empty traditions or habitual practices and gives almost no thought to fresh expressions of biblical mandates.

Perhaps God wants something different. Perhaps He intends a pastor's dedication to grow a great soul to help a congregation clarify its mission. It may also help illuminate God's will for a specific church at a particular time. The pastor's personal prayer efforts often ignite his ability to share his vision.

A 35-year-old pastor who served a small church for more than five years explains: "When my Scripture reading and intercessory prayer keep me close to God, I sometimes experience a pastoral guidance system, something like ESP, or perhaps it is more like radar. I am aware of what God wants done when and sometimes why. In trying to follow this guidance, I am in error often enough that I do not blame Him for false impressions, but I have been guided enough times that I always act upon those directions."

Another minister describes a similar link: "I get specific assignments for ministry at old First Church when I pray and read Scripture. My prayer conversations invigorate my ministry. To my delight, I receive up-to-date prescriptions from the Physician of my soul."

What provides more satisfaction than having God's guidance as to how mission is to be carried out in a particular setting? How exhilarating to draw close to God so we experience His blank-check promise that He will draw close to us!

Personal Spiritual Growth Leads Us Along Well-Marked Trails

Spiritual formation generally makes use of established disciplines of the inner life. The disciplines take us along trails that saints have walked in all generations. However, something incredibly new is frequently discovered by the wide-awake pilgrim.

A hiking path in our neighborhood offers a good example. Our trail, paved and predictable, even has mileage markers, along with a spectacular view of Pikes Peak. Spring wild flowers and winter snow showers sometimes decorate the path. But the view is different each time I walk the trail because the sun changes the light so often.

Growing a great soul is like that. Although there are many familiar landmarks along the paths of righteousness, new richness keeps showing up as one travels these well-known trails. God keeps infusing eternal truth with new light and brighter color and richer texture.

Personal Spiritual Growth Prevents "Inner Kill"
Cynicism and distrust all add up to a climate of suspicion in our society. This attitude frequently seeps into the church and causes what one psychologist calls "inner kill" in the pastor's soul. This graphic phrase offers an accurate assessment of what happens when a pastor suffers from dulled motivation or from superficial faith over long periods.

Prolonged scarcity of fulfillment intensifies "inner kill" for people in any profession, especially pastors. Playing it safe also destroys drive and initiative. Inner resurrection, one of God's amazing specialties, is the remedy. "Inner kill" thrives when a pastor curbs the prophetic directives of Scripture, when he sees his situation as hopeless or when he fails to find adventure in ministry. The fallout causes him to mark time, to mire him in a time warp or to distort his priorities.

To prevent this condition, the minister's spirituality must be intentionally personal and much more than a professionalized piety. Frail spiritual weaklings won't do for pastors.

Personal Spiritual Growth Heals Harmful Experiences
One pastor describes his struggles, as he works out his spiritual fitness, in these words:

"I was raised in a household where prayer was used to manipulate and restrict life. I had to go through a time of rebellion before I could come to know another kind of prayer, but I still can identify with feelings that make those who have been raised in the church turn away from religious words and practices. They have been turned off by the unreality of much of it."[7] How devastating and distressing that anyone would even unknowingly pervert prayer for another, especially a child.

Unfortunate or counterfeit childhood experiences, however bad they seem or harmful their influence, do not invalidate our need for the holy.

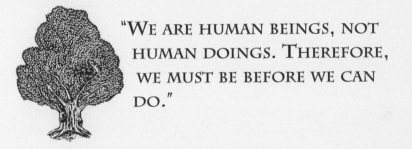

"WE ARE HUMAN BEINGS, NOT HUMAN DOINGS. THEREFORE, WE MUST BE BEFORE WE CAN DO."

A person cannot give up knowing Jesus intimately as the central force for ministry just because childhood religious experiences were not ideal or because of a few bizarre Christians.

Personal Spiritual Growth Restores Balance

Pastoral ministry has many confusing expectations that originate from various sources. All these changing demands easily get us off balance. Conflicting priorities hound us continually. Expectations confuse us, too—theirs, ours and God's. Thus, every reflective pastor is frequently bothered by his use of time and by the fact that ministry is never finished. That being true, where does the possibility for balance come from? The priority issue must be addressed if a pastor is to grow a great soul.

When a pastor prays and listens carefully to Scripture, he sees being and doing as two interrelated dimensions of ministry. Each informs the other. A student underscored this interplay on her Bible college senior exam, "We are human beings, not human doings. Therefore, we must be before we can do." Thus, when an activist pastor listens to God, he sees character flaws in himself that his Father wants corrected and healed.

Conversely, the introspective pastor, while reading the Holy Book and praying, feels sent into a more active involvement in the lives of people. This built-in creative tension between being and doing nurtures growth. Contemplative praying and redemptive doing are two sides of the same coin of ministry that must be constantly polished in a pastor's spiritual development.

Denominations, special interest groups and local congregations need to be introduced to this message again. Without spiritual energy, religious activism is nothing more than a round of beneficent activities that quickly run out of purpose and passion and support.

The opposite also is true. Christians who give their whole attention to personal character development can become so heavenly minded that they are of no earthly good.

Pastors who carefully listen to Scripture, prayer and the devotional giants find resources for building such a delightful balance between being and doing. Thus, they will hear the call of the people in the streets while cultivating their inner world. On the other hand, they will hear a call to be like their Master in the noise, the hurry and the crowd. This process of balancing being and doing stretches a pastor between rationality and spontaneity, grit and grace, piety and practicability, obligation and gladness, faith and fun.

EIGHT WAYS TO GROW A GREAT SOUL

To cultivate an effective, fulfilling ministry, let's get specific about how to grow a great soul. Try to view spiritual fitness as more than a high-octane spiritual additive to be poured into the details of ministry. Think of growing a great soul, rather, as nothing more or nothing less than an authentic Christian life—normal, whole, well-adjusted and Jesus-focused—that is lived as God intends us to live.

Inasmuch as spiritual growth can come from any activity or action that draws us nearer to God, this list is merely suggestive and not exhaustive.

1. Cultivate a Soul Friend
Every pastor needs an absolutely trustworthy friend to whom he voluntarily makes himself spiritually accountable. Ideally, a soul friend freely

questions a pastor about his motives, his marriage and his ministry. The soul friend must be given permission to question a pastor about his relationship with God.

A pastor needs a soul friend who loves him enough to be tender, yet tough. He needs someone to pray for him and with him. Ideally, the soul friend should be willing to listen redemptively to his hurts, to affirm his strengths and to call him to authenticity. He must know when to pat the pastor on the back and when to kick him in the seat. This person should be his best friend and his most demanding critic.

2. Resist the Seduction of Safety

Mere maintenance in church attendance, fund-raising or personal spiritual development sounds so good to us. Humanly, we want to hold onto what we have developed or inherited. It's good, we feel, to be safe.

In fact, one high-placed leader always would ask me about every potential recruit or new program, "Is he/it safe?" He rejected progressive ideas because they might be controversial, and he seldom appointed maverick ministers because they were too threatening. To the detriment of the Kingdom, he often missed the energy and achievement of new ideas and of innovative people.

We are often like that, too. Our reluctance to risk, to pioneer new frontiers or to reinvent ministry hinders the work of God and makes it mediocre and inane. The word "great," as in growing a great soul, frightens us. It is so much easier to be careful and cautious and predictable— all words that do not seem to fit in the same paragraph with the gospel, missions and worldwide impact.

3. Solicit Prayers from the Faithful

Stamina strengthens ministry that is undergirded by prayer. Untapped prayer support surrounds us. We have more people than we realize who are interested in praying for us. We can have more prayer for the asking, and most of us need all the prayer we can get. Think of those people who might be willing to take your ministry to the Father.

People who nurtured your faith. Sunday School teachers, pastors and friends in your home church will feel highly honored if you ask them to pray for you every day. Power from these prayers cannot be hindered by miles or clocks or calendars.

People whom you have served in crises. Every person you helped through a crisis is a prospective candidate to support your ministry with prayer. Because of difficulties you shared with them, they have a built-in awareness of how much you need supernatural assistance as you seek to serve others just as you served them. They are bonded to you forever by the tender compassion you once showed them.

People who need attention. Every congregation has people who need and want more attention than a pastor is able to give them. A common example is shut-ins who regret they do not get more of their pastor's time. They may be frail or sick and believe they are unneeded because they cannot do what they once enjoyed doing in the church. Their limitations make them feel useless. Consequently, asking them to pray for you turns their focus to significant concerns outside themselves and makes them feel needed again. It involves them in something important they can do and something you need. Everyone gains.

People who serve with you. Christian workers can expect to receive magnificent power when they band together in prayer support for a common cause. Examples are the devotional periods at Focus on the Family headquarters in Colorado Springs, a local church staff meeting for daily prayer and a church board gathering early Sunday morning to intercede for the ministry of that day.

Try enlisting committee members of your church to covenant to pray for each other every day. Emphasize this need as being more important than agenda decisions. As a result, a spiritual synergism develops so two do much more than twice what you can do alone.

Ministry peers can share prayers. At the top of all the inspirational sentences I have ever received in a letter were the words, "Let's trade prayers." What an energetic enabling force for ministry.

4. Rekindle Affection for the Bible
Allow the Bible to shape you. Saturate your life with Scripture by active Bible reading. Let your encounter with the Bible shape the details of your ministry. Enter into mental conversation with Bible characters. Synchronize

your thinking with its message so you hear, respond and apply new truths to this moment of your life. Use Scripture to energize your ministry.

Read for relevance. Be open to insight about your life and ministry. Develop a continuous friendship with the Author. Go for quality as well as for quantity. Listen closely to what the Spirit is saying. What does God want you to hear through Scripture about your service for Him?

Interrogate Scripture. Walk around its message and meaning. Check similar ideas in various passages by using a concordance and commentaries. Probe the passage. Explore, research, study, compare and contrast. As you read, ask questions about how this passage affects your life.

Personalize the passage. Put your name in a promise or a command. What affirmation does Scripture say about your ministry? Does it seem to have your name and zip code written into it? If you were present at a particular biblical event, what would you feel and what would you do?

⑤ Grow Past Your Prayer Hang-Ups

I (Neil) love the old story about lightning striking a night club in a tiny western town after the Christian people had an all-night prayer meeting, asking God to destroy the "den of iniquity." When the night-club owner heard about the prayer meeting, he sued the church. Immediately the church people denied any responsibility. The judge threw the case out of court after he observed, "Apparently the night club owner believes in prayer more than the church people." This is an interesting parable for pastors.

Like other believers, pastors sometimes suffer from prayer hang-ups. As a result, they major on their problems about prayer without experiencing its possibilities. Most of us have at least one or more prayer dilemmas, but a single obstacle should not keep us from earnest conversations with our Lord.

Unanswered prayers cause stumbling blocks. Although we do not have much light on why some prayers are not answered, God has proven Himself to be the dependable one. Therefore, why not pray in an act of intentional Christian commitment, "I trust You even though I do not understand why a particular prayer was not answered. I love You. And I want to serve You all the days of my life, both in the storm as well as in the sunshine."

Delayed answers often seem unnecessary, even cruel. However, because God knows tomorrow as well as He knows yesterday and today, His wait-awhile answer is always best. Remember that delay does not mean denial.

Guilt about not praying more stalks many good people. In their inwardness, many people carry a picture of God as a harsh, heavenly timekeeper who inspects their time cards every day. They believe God would be more pleased if they prayed longer and louder. Of course, we all could pray more, but the quality of our relationship with God affects our prayers, too. To stop praying because we did not pray enough last week or last month does not move us nearer to God.

Unrelinquished concerns cannot be changed. Every genuine believer some-times feels handcuffed by people or issues he cannot control or change. These concerns may perhaps be the consequences of past sins.

Then, too, people from our past have complicated our lives in ways we cannot shake. Some feel defeated by lies told about them, even by good people. Some have been cheated by duplicity or outright stealing. Others have been locked out of what might have been by parents or by spouses or by children. A victorious relinquishment of these concerns will liberate us to live a satisfying life and to have an improved ministry. This may be the precise time to pray for that victory—take your hands off for all time.

6. Enjoy God

Many believers dread spending time with God. They are afraid because they think of Him as an authoritative judge, accusing parent, perfection-istic professor, unbending boss or absentee landlord. Accordingly, their meetings with God are dreadfully unpleasant.

If we want to grow a great soul, however, it is essential to whole-heartedly embrace the fact that God champions us. More than the most loving human parent, God wants us to succeed so we can find joy in ser-vice and do our adventuresome part to advance His kingdom.

Recently, I (Neil) heard a pastor tell about an early-morning appoint-ment he kept with God. Being a night person, he has difficulty getting up. After dragging himself out of bed to pray on a particular morning, he started back to bed with sleepy eyes and a sluggish brain. Then he experienced an impression as real as an audible voice: "So you would rather sleep another hour than keep your appointment with Me. Who would miss for anything in the whole world a meeting with the King of the Universe, the Lord of resurrection life and the Lover of your soul?" God's friendly chastisement transformed the pastor's devotional duty into winsome fellowship with the Father.

Ministry, by definition, makes us partners with omnipotence. Even though we are junior partners, we are important, needed and essential. The mental pictures we have of God provide affirming inspiration we too easily overlook:

- *The Judge* sets us free when we deserve imprisonment or death.
- *The Parent* affirms us as a member of God's family.
- *The Professor* teaches us truth about the world and ourselves.
- As Sovereign Lord, Jesus is *the Ruler* of all life. And as *the Landowner*, He provides shelter, security and warmth.

Although the possibilities of enjoying the Father are thoroughly rooted in Scripture, the Westminster Catechism summarizes it in beautiful shorthand language. It asks, "What is the chief end of humankind?" and it answers, "To glorify God and enjoy God forever."

Look for ways to enjoy God continually. Discover fun and fascination and exhilaration in prayers, Scripture reading, people to whom you minister, hymns and the magnificent examples of grace all around you. Great souls enjoy the sparkle and satisfaction of friendship with God and His people. Cultivate a sense of joyful ministry for the sheer adventure of it.

Take the glumness out of ministry for a week and it might never return. It is essential that every minister build an enjoyable relationship with God into the fabric of every pastoral effort. Pastoring links us with God's mighty power. Let's act like it.

7. Pray Risky and Adventuresome Prayers

Some prayers seem like tough exams that show us what we do not know, what the professor expects and significant issues we have overlooked.

Spiritual directors and devotional saints across centuries have cautioned believers against prayers that request miracles with no effort on their part. Prayers are generally not answered that way.

Far from being magic formulas, prayers are usually answered by receiving an assignment that can be achieved only with divine aid. God answers prayers by empowering us after we have done our best.

Human experience offers many examples. You will have your patience tested when you pray for patience. You will be given a peacemaking task when you petition for peace. Pray for generosity and God will ask you to give more than you have ever given. In a similar vein, genuinely great sermons usually grow out of human anguish or even travail before they receive divine anointing.

Here are five risky and adventuresome prayers that will add a supernatural dimension to your ministry, that will send you into specialized tasks, that will shape you into Christlikeness or that will require more than your best efforts. These prayers could change your ministry forever:

- Search me.
- Break me.
- Stretch me.
- Lead me.
- Use me.

Seldom does a person pray even one of these petitions without incredible growth happening in his inner relationship with God or in his outer expressions of Kingdom service. These petitions produce authentic achievement in the front lines of ministry.

(8) Commit to Spiritual Self-Care

Adequate spiritual self-care is a little-understood secret of a flourishing ministry. To adequately care for his own spiritual fitness, a pastor must buck busy schedules, priority pressures, unreasonable expectations and secular values. But it must be done.

Like everyone else, pastors should desire the best possible life. That life is Christ-directed living centered on our Lord's teachings, energized by His nearness and steeped in His will. The center of a minister's responsibility is to find such a life for himself and then to share it with those he serves. Thus, self-care multiplies ministry rather than being a favor he does only for himself.

Seeking such a satisfying life may be the main reason people come to church week after week. Sadly, many seekers believe it is a spiritual mirage or an unobtainable ideal because such a Christ-quality life is so seldom modeled before them. Perhaps more people would want this valuable life if we reminded them that Christ brings eternal newness to people of every

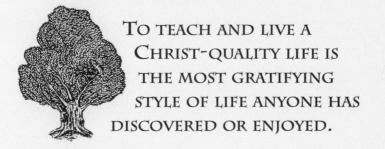

To teach and live a Christ-quality life is the most gratifying style of life anyone has discovered or enjoyed.

generation as it welcomes Him into the details of their lives. Perhaps more people would thirst for such a quality life if the Church did not keep faith safely embalmed in ancient words or yesteryear's creeds. We have the privilege to show them authentic Christian living at its best.

Shout it from the housetops and live it in the streets; nothing faintly compares with the Jesus way of life. The people we serve will be significantly affected by its relevance and sweetness as they observe it working well in our songs, in our catastrophes, in our ambiguities and in our victories. Remember: To teach and live a Christ-quality life is the most gratifying style of life anyone has discovered or enjoyed.

Too many pastors feel their personal spiritual development is hindered by problems, difficulties or limitations. Sometimes they blame their shallowness on a power-hungry matriarch or patriarch in the congregation. But a pastor must look past every impediment to realize a Christ-quality life can be cultivated anywhere. Even tough pastoral assignments offer enough stretching points and affirmative influences for a pastor and spouse to build a Jesus-permeated life.

To nourish this kind of life, a pastor must realize continuously that he is a grace consumer, not a producer. To make it happen for himself, a pastor must value and celebrate the momentous serendipities of pastoral service. Reading, praying and knowing God are part of his job description, something very different from the occupational demands of average Harry in the parish.

Self-care is not only beneficial for the pastor, however, but the congregation also benefits. Such bonding with Christ deepens a pastor's devotion to ministry and helps him portray Christlikeness in the expressions of his ministry. It positively affects his preaching, counseling and worship leadership. A holy contagion will then ignite his congregation.

As a result, church members move nearer to Christ because they see spiritual adventure at work in their minister. As they see the life of Christ embodied in their leader, their spiritual appetites increase. They begin thirsting for a life of love and trust and grace. This spiritual interplay between pastor and laity is spiritual blooming at its best.

However, without vibrant personal spiritual self-care, a pastor sentences himself to leading a well-intended religious business enterprise, a do-goodish relief agency or an affable social club. That's not much fun, and it produces a boring life.

A GREAT SOUL REVITALIZES MINISTRY

Grow a great soul so that supernatural strengths of character will enrich and energize every expression of your ministry. Our personal spiritual strengths can become a mighty combined force for curing the discord and disharmony and confusion that prevail in the Church and in society.

Therefore, fill your inner life with the spirit of Jesus so His character shows in your ministry. Then the work of Christ under your leadership will survive and thrive as well as flourish.

- Great souls *preach* powerfully, warmly and redemptively.
- Great souls *care* for hurting, broken people and point them to the Savior.

- Great souls *lead* worshipers into God's awesome presence.
- Great souls *build* strong families, cherish their marriages and see the Church as the family of God.
- Great souls substitute supernatural achievement for cheap, empty talk.

Consider the incredible possibilities. God intends that ministry will profoundly affect those you serve. But He plans much more. God wants your ministry to shape you into Christlikeness and to add adventure to your life in ways beyond your fondest imagination. Ministry takes you to adventuresome places you would never go without it. Ministry allows you to rub shoulders with and to influence people you would otherwise never know. Your junior partnership with God allows you privileges and permits you to receive grace in a measure no one experiences in other occupations.

Genuine greatness expands your credibility and kindles your passion for Christ. Growing a great soul blasts away the corrosion that, like acid, eats away at the Church's achievement and vision. A thousand pastors with growing souls can rekindle fires of principle, hope, devotion, conviction, magnanimity, servanthood, imagination, creativity and holy living.

CONTEMPORARY CHALLENGE
HOW TO KEEP IN SHAPE SPIRITUALLY

- Go beyond a professionalized ministry to a personal pilgrimage with God.
- View ministry as a colossal opportunity to grow a great soul.

- Apply to yourself principles of spiritual wellness that you preach to others.
- Refuse to allow your own spirituality to become ceremonial.
- Renew the adventure of being a spokesperson for the resurrected Lord.
- Model the God-permeated life.
- Balance your ministry between being and doing.
- Resist the seduction of safety.
- Solicit prayers from the faithful.
- Enjoy God.

In the middle of the bad, it has never been so good!
—Student Prayer[8]

Notes

1. John Henry Jowett, *The Preacher and His Work* (New York: Doran and Company, 1912), p. 45.
2. Alexander Solzhenitsyn, *Christianity Today*, Sept. 13, 1993, p. 96.
3. Eugene H. Petersen, *Working the Angles* (Grand Rapids, MI: Wm. B. Eerdmans Publishing, 1987), p. 2.
4. Ibid., p. 3.
5. T. S. Eliot, *Choruses from "The Rock," Collected Poems, 1909-1929* (New York: Harcourt, Brace and World, Inc., 1930).
6. Derf Bergman, "Sermon Preparation by Doing," *Circuit Rider*, September 1993, p. 17.
7. Elizabeth O'Conner, *Journey Inward, Journey Outward* (New York: HarperCollins, 1968), p. 12.
8. Henri Nouwen, *Intimacy* (San Francisco: HarperSanFrancisco, 1969), p. 59.

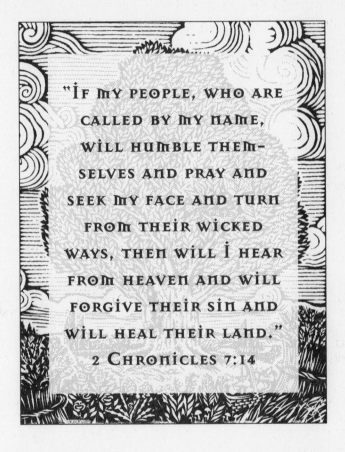

"IF MY PEOPLE, WHO ARE
CALLED BY MY NAME,
WILL HUMBLE THEM-
SELVES AND PRAY AND
SEEK MY FACE AND TURN
FROM THEIR WICKED
WAYS, THEN WILL I HEAR
FROM HEAVEN AND WILL
FORGIVE THEIR SIN AND
WILL HEAL THEIR LAND."
2 CHRONICLES 7:14

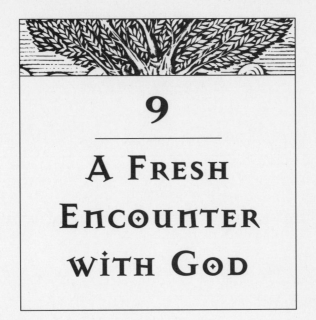

9

A FRESH ENCOUNTER WITH GOD

Father, send revival and renewal to my soul and church.
Invigorate, rejuvenate and revitalize every phase of my ministry.
Help me live by the reality that I can do nothing without You.
Amen.

"IT'S ME, IT'S ME, O LORD"

"A few members of any church must get thoroughly right with God," was evangelist Dr. R. A. Torrey's first rule for revival. However, if a pastor is serious about renewal in his ministry and church, the rule must be personalized with his name and address and zip code.

Then the rule reads, "Let (insert your name) get thoroughly right with God as a first step of revival." To reinforce the revival rule we sing, "It's me, it's me, O Lord, standing in the need of prayer."

The supernatural power of personal revival is illustrated in the following testimony that I (H. B.) shared at a pastor's conference.

Pastor Shares His Need of Renewal

A life-changing renewal came to me after I had been a pastor for 15 years in Salem, Oregon. I was a pastor of a spiritually vibrant church, but I still saw myself as a phony. I went through the right motions without the right motives. I saw myself accomplishing about what anyone could do if given the same opportunities. My success, however, was not comfort enough. I needed healing, revival.

One night in a dark, silent church when no one was present, I fell across the altar in a mood of spiritual desperation. I began to pray the most humiliating prayer you could imagine.

I prayed, "O God, I want out of this. I want out of the ministry. I'm not worthy of this church. I'm artificial and a play actor. You need to get me out of this. I would appreciate it if you could get me out gracefully. But if it is not graceful, that's okay, too. I just can't go on with this pain inside."

At that point, I humbled myself. I admitted to God that I was not authentic. I acknowledged that I was inadequate. I confessed that I was an unworthy vessel, full of cracks and holes. I admitted that I was running on spiritual empty.

At that moment, the presence of Christ came over me with empowerment and meaning. The Lord seemed to say in that moment, "Now I can use you." The results of that encounter with the Lord changed my whole life. It revolutionized my ministry.

Personalizing Torrey's rule may seem a bit uncomfortable at first. But spiritual development never works for "them" before it starts with "us," for "me." Like so many things in ministry, revival is a matter of leadership, priority and visibility.

From what you know about God and about how churches function, you know that few congregations will become spiritual powerhouses until their pastors first experience a fresh personal encounter with God. Consequently, the first step for authentic revival is personal renewal of the pastor at any cost.

The second step follows the first automatically. A genuine spiritual awakening causes a pastor to feel a holy dissatisfaction with things as they are. Thousands of ministers who become fed up must speak up in kindly but unmistakable ways about what needs to be changed.

Our legitimate discontent centers around playing church, coddling emotional infants, worrying about personal security, preaching arid doctrinal scholasticism, baby-sitting trivia, being controlled by spiritual pygmies and living by savage schedules that leave no time for prayer, study or outreach.

It's time to face the fact that the nation's moral malaise and the Church's navel-gazing apathy are sobering, serious spiritual issues. It's time to seek reality in knowing God, to fast, to receive God's perspective and to insist upon authenticity in ourselves and in church leaders above and below us. It's time to get serious about holy living so that it becomes a personal and congregational obsession.

It's time to move beyond puny image building about small successes to accomplishing truly supernatural exploits for God—the kind that transform individuals and revolutionize society. It's time to rally all the church's facilities, finances and personnel to win the war against evil and godlessness.

For such a revival, we must pray Habakkuk's prayer for ourselves, our assignments, our denominations, our colleges and our publishing houses, "O Lord, revive thy work!" And we must march and sing:

> O Breath of Life, come sweeping through us;
> Revive Thy Church with life and power.
> O Breath of Life, come, cleanse, renew us;
> And fit Thy Church to meet this hour.[1]

MAKE REVIVAL A USER-FRIENDLY WORD

Revivals have a bad reputation in many places. Because a spurt of religious enthusiasm soon plays out, it is argued that planned and calendared revivals accomplish little. The conclusion seems overly jaded, however, when you consider that some renewal is better than none. A Methodist bishop said in a conversation where revival meetings were being criticized, "I agree that revivals are often ineffective, but that's how I got into the Kingdom."

The revival we need will take us back to the basics of faith and reactivate a no-reservations commitment to the cause of Christ. Such a revival will require us to humble our souls before God, to question our ego and to get serious about personal righteousness. Such a revival will stimulate fresh love and soul-stretching adoration for Christ and will energize selfless service to God and neighbor.

Such a contagious revival will make the life of God satisfying, joyful and fun again. And it will anoint our preaching with a holy contagion so we are able to make the gospel inviting and invigorating to a broken world.

Norman Vincent Peale paints a clear picture of the kind of revival we seek when he described his father's ministry as a revivalist, "What he [Peale's father] wanted was in-depth life-change in which not only emotion but the mind combined in a commitment bringing spiritual growth and lifelong Christian discipleship."[2]

That's real revival—an in-depth life-changing commitment involving the emotions and mind that makes believers in our churches and we ourselves spiritually different and growing for a lifetime.

Look Beyond the Wrappings
More slick substitutes, maneuvering manipulation or extreme emotionalism is not what we desire from revivals out of the past. Rather, it is the God of revival and renewal we seek.

Like stories from our childhood, it's fun to retell revival experiences from our past. I remember an evangelist who displayed an open casket with a mirror in place of a corpse at the front of the church. I recall singing 34 verses of "Just as I Am." In college years, I remember being tricked into admitting in public that I had not surrendered to Christ.

In my mind, I can still see eccentric evangelists out of the past with big cars, garish ties, giant Bibles and flashy suits. Those itinerants sometimes sold study Bibles, records, books or ceramic eagles to help them making a living. But these are just the wrappings. There is so much more to real revival.

Let's try looking past the externals to the essential. What is the essential nature of revival? What is the driving force for authentic revival?

For real revival to take place, God wants a minister and a church to thoroughly examine their relationship to Christ and to continually evaluate ministry in light of Kingdom priorities. Depth and obedience are to replace shallowness and play acting. God intends for revival to impact the heart of a pastor and the heart of a congregation.

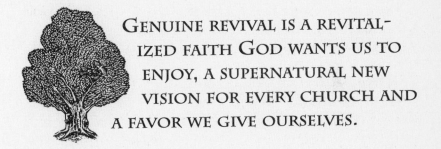

GENUINE REVIVAL IS A REVITALIZED FAITH GOD WANTS US TO ENJOY, A SUPERNATURAL NEW VISION FOR EVERY CHURCH AND A FAVOR WE GIVE OURSELVES.

For an individual, such a renewing welcomes God into the citadel of the soul. It joyously allows a loving Father to forgive outward sin and remedy inner corruption. Genuine revival makes us willing to turn from sin, rebellion and disobedience. Genuine renewal requires humbling one's self, seeking God's face, turning from wicked ways and changing in any way He suggests. Real revival helps us make the wonderful trade of giving up embarrassing self-sovereignty to receive God's guidance, grace and will.

Follow Scriptural Directions

From Genesis to Revelation, the Bible is a book about reality and renewal and starting again. It encourages us to eagerly hope for revival, and it commands us to earnestly seek revival. We are to yearn for renewal as if it all comes from God. At the same time, we are to seek renewal as if its coming depends completely on us.

Scripture teaches that revival is more than a desirable wish or an idealized spiritual state of being. Rather, genuine revival is a revitalized faith

God wants us to enjoy, a supernatural new vision for every church and a favor we give ourselves.

Consider these scriptural directives for seeking authentic revival and for kindling genuine renewal.

Peter proclaims the necessity. At Pentecost, Peter proclaimed revival ingredients, "Repent, then, and turn to God, so that your sins may be wiped out, that times of refreshing may come from the Lord, and that he may send the Christ, who has been appointed for you—even Jesus" (Acts 3:19,20).

Jesus explains the source of revival. Even after two centuries have passed, Jesus' immortal words at the Feast of Tabernacles still call the Church to authentic renewal, "If anyone is thirsty, let him come to me and drink. Whoever believes in me, as the Scripture has said, streams of living water will flow from within him" (John 7:37,38).

Revival impacts a nation. Scripture teaches a connection between a genuine revival of God's people and the spiritual salvaging of a nation. In the events surrounding the dedication of the Temple, this connection between the people of God and their nation appears at least twice.

Solomon prayed earnestly for God to honor their worship in the new location with His presence:

> When your people Israel have been defeated by an enemy because they have sinned against you and when they turn back and confess your name, praying and making supplication before you in this temple, then hear from heaven and forgive the sin of your people Israel and bring them back to the land you gave to them and their fathers (2 Chron. 6:24,25).

Note the relationship of the land to Israel's sinfulness.

Places of worship need the reviving presence of God. Solomon understood that it is possible to build a magnificent house of worship without much of God's presence. Solomon also knew he could never revive himself. His seeking after God shows he agreed with Charles Spurgeon, who wrote centuries later, "You would just as soon expect a wounded soldier on the battlefield to heal himself without medicine, or get himself to a hospital when his arms and legs have been shot off as you would expect to revive yourself without the help of God."³

After the Temple was completed, God answered Solomon's prayer, "If my people, who are called by my name, will humble themselves and pray and seek my face and turn from their wicked ways, then will I hear from heaven and will forgive their sin and will heal their land" (2 Chron. 7:14). A common theme keeps appearing: Although revival comes from God, we have an important role in bringing it to pass.

John gave God's formula for revival. A pattern for revival is clearly spelled out in the apostle John's warning to the Church at Ephesus. He begins by complimenting the noble achievements of the congregation. He commends them for good deeds, hard work, persevering tenacity, refusal to follow false apostles and willingness to endure hardships. This list of admirable qualities is desirable for any church!

"Yet..."

"Yet, you have forsaken your first love." All their impressive achievements had little significance without a return to their first love. After issuing a solemn warning, John tells the Ephesian church members they will be renewed if they (1) remember the heights from which they have fallen; (2) repent; and (3) repeat the things they did at the beginning (see Rev. 2:1-6).

The warning, intended especially for the Ephesians, also applies to us: "He who has an ear, let him hear what the Spirit says to the churches" (Rev. 2:7). A first love lost is the problem, and rediscovering first love is the solution.

The ancient prophet has a demanding word, too. A renewal passage in Hosea speaks to contemporary churches: "Sow for yourselves righteousness, reap the fruit of unfailing love, and break up your unplowed ground; for it is time to seek the Lord, until he comes and showers righteousness on you" (Hos. 10:12).

Many Churches Need a Heart Warming

Many churches are orthodox in doctrine and are busy in worthwhile activity but, like the Ephesians, have lost their first love. Some of these churches have pastors who know Scripture well and preach sermons decked out in impressive scholarship, generously seasoned with secular self-help suggestions. But something is missing, so neither pastors nor parishes glow with childlike faith, unpretentious obedience and holy joy.

Because of lost love, outsiders regrettably find little warmth or nourishment in these fellowships. Years ago, Baptist evangelist Vance Havner described our current situation in words that sound like this morning's newspaper, "While we cry out against liberalism and loose living, are we not blind to the perils of lukewarmness?...Call it what you will, we need a heart-warming."[4]

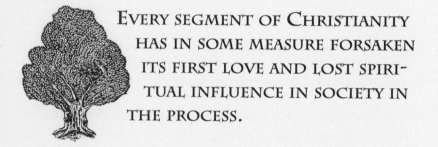

EVERY SEGMENT OF CHRISTIANITY HAS IN SOME MEASURE FORSAKEN ITS FIRST LOVE AND LOST SPIRITUAL INFLUENCE IN SOCIETY IN THE PROCESS.

Today, some churches toy, or even trifle, with revival. Like a small child with a short attention span on Christmas morning, many contemporary churches keep checking the ecclesiastical smorgasbord of the latest fads, looking for easier ways to do ministry. Magic quick-fix programs that cost little soul passion and require less commitment are sought.

Sometimes, an entire congregation tries to make itself believe that a religious performance is an actual revival or that an overly energetic worship service is genuine renewal. Performance, great crowds and noise are not in themselves useful criteria. It is amazingly easy to fool ourselves into believing we are being renewed, when inside we are dried up.

Most of this is like fool's gold—a shoddy substitute for the real thing. Inside we are dying for a fresh infilling of God. Inside we are dry and barren and a long way from what God wants us to be.

Ministry Is a Dangerous Occupation
I recently talked with an insurance underwriter who ranks pastors among the safest actuarial risks a life insurance company can have from a phys-

ical point of view. Yet, ministry can be among the most dangerous of all occupations spiritually.

The cause of this risk, of course, is the enemy of our souls who ambushes ministers with sly snares and subtle temptations. An ineffective, compromised or fallen pastor makes the devil's labors easier and more convincing. The enemy gets more credit than he deserves. Often our problems are self-induced by neglected prayer life, self-sufficiency or professional pride.

The prophetic words written by Charles Spurgeon in the last century should cause us to stand at full spiritual attention:

> We too often flog the church when the whip should be laid
> on our own shoulders. We should always remember that we
> are a part of the church, and that our own lack of revival is
> in some measure the cause of the lack of revival in the
> church at large. I will lay the charge before us; we ministers
> need a revival of piety in our lives. I have abundant grounds
> to prove it.[5]

REVIVALS START WITH HOLY DISSATISFACTION

Earlier in this chapter, we considered how God builds the need of revival and the hope for renewal into the fabric of Scripture. Scripture frequently warns us about the tendency of spiritual fire going out.

It reminds us, too, that organized religion nearly always continues its rituals and rules and regulations long after it has lost its soul. But in six words, John the apostle clinches the truth and stops all our defenses, "You have forsaken your first love."

Regardless of our theological label—evangelicals, liberals, conservatives, independents, charismatics, Catholics, reformed, Calvinists, Wesleyans—we all know John is right. The Church's first love has been forsaken. Incriminating evidence is everywhere. Every segment of Christianity has in some measure forsaken its first love and lost spiritual influence in society in the process.

How bad will it get before every pastor personally begins to stir up holy dissatisfaction with the way things are in his own soul and in the church?

Dissatisfaction 1: Loss of First Love

A long time ago, a ministry examination board asked a student pastor, "What does repentance mean?"

The young man replied, "To have a godly sorrow for sin."

The chairman of the examination board said, "You are only partly right. Repentance means to have a godly sorrow for sin, but it also means a willingness to forsake one's sins forever."

Sorrow and a willingness to forsake are important directives for the modern church. The Church in general, and local congregations in particular, have many reasons to repent. You can list your own convincing reasons. But even a very short list must include confused priorities, lukewarmness, shallowness, sin, diluted message and inappropriate use of monies contributed for ministry.

For too long, contemporary congregations have given themselves high marks because they worked hard, persevered and refused to follow false prophets. But John clearly told the Ephesians that was good, but not good enough for God. The church at Ephesus did those things well, and John still called them to repentance and insisted that they needed to return to their first love (see Rev. 2:1-6).

Dissatisfaction 2: Leaders with Sin in Their Lives

A church is never what God wants it to be when those who lead are living in sin. God's holy standards apply to laity and clergy equally. To the Corinthians, Paul wrote about sexual immorality in the church, "And you are proud! Shouldn't you rather have been filled with grief and have put out of your fellowship the man who did this?" (1 Cor. 5:2).

In God's expectations for His Church, willful sin disqualifies a person for leadership. The Father's serious concerns likely include sins we do not often worry about in church leaders such as lying, cheating, doublespeak, gossip, stealing and greed.

Biblical standards of the holy life must be applied to all who lead the

Church in any way. Otherwise the Church becomes a sham and pretense and travesty in the eyes of her people and the community. Teachers, singers, decision makers, worship leaders, praise-team members, all must live lives that are pleasing to God and inspiring to the congregation.

Pastors must rid their churches of sin. It must be done carefully, redemptively and tenderly, but it must be done. Too often people, because their talent is so badly needed, are allowed to lead when they are spiritually unqualified. But yieldedness to Christ is the first key to Kingdom service and not talent alone.

Six facts must be faced in dealing with sin in leaders:

- God wants leaders to be holy.
- People in the pews know more about a leader's lifestyles than we think.
- Spiritually unqualified leaders often get right with God when a pastor urges change.
- If spiritual charades are allowed to continue, the offenders may eventually lose their souls.
- Spiritually unqualified leaders generally create an unwholesome drag on a church's ministry.
- Outsiders may never come to church because they know leaders are not living as they should.

Dissatisfaction 3: The Church Becomes Worldly Minded

Worldliness chooses secular values rather than Kingdom priorities. Worldliness allows sophistication, security and self-sovereignty to press us into secular ways of thinking and acting. Worldliness is playacting, leaving the impression of being holy, separate and devoted when we are not.

For 2,000 years, the Church has crippled itself when it allowed the spirit and values of the world to shape its ministry. For some sad reason, each new generation has to learn this lesson. The secular world and a spiritual church do not mix any better than oil and water.

Worldliness sometimes shows in churches as a group pride of achievement or pride of spiritual commitment or pride of worship practices.

Pride of achievement has been the downfall of churches who allow themselves to be distracted by their prominence, talent or even their missionary efforts. In the process, some great old churches and some contemporary emerging congregations have become only an echo of what they
could be in the kingdom of Christ.

Some congregations pride themselves in their piety. Being superspiri-
tual, these churches easily drift into becoming a holy club that admits

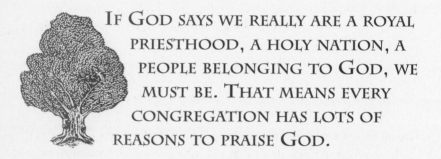

> IF GOD SAYS WE REALLY ARE A ROYAL
> PRIESTHOOD, A HOLY NATION, A
> PEOPLE BELONGING TO GOD, WE
> MUST BE. THAT MEANS EVERY
> CONGREGATION HAS LOTS OF
> REASONS TO PRAISE GOD.

only those who act and look a certain way—usually some weird way.
They are separate for the sake of being separate but fail to realize that
spiritual pride is actually sly self-deceiving worldliness.

Worship practices also can become a subtle form of worldliness for
churches. Some churches are proud of worn-out worship forms that no
longer inspire anyone or that are little understood. Other churches are
proud, believing they are special to God because of the energy, enthusiasm or noise level of their services. Why the pride in either extreme?
Worship forms are nothing more than channels to help people into the
presence of God; forms are never an end in themselves.

Worldliness can also infect a church's methods. In a day of shifting par-
adigms with many innovative ways of thinking and doing, many church
leaders assume any method that is new or produces visible results is acceptable to God. A not-so-holy pragmatism sometimes makes us believe any
means justifies the end, when the means and the end often need to be
reevaluated in light of the New Testament. Although worldliness may not
be in the method, it can be in the attitude of those who use the method.

Dissatisfaction 4: A Church Loses Its Sense of Wonder
Your church has amazing reasons to praise God. According to Peter, "But you are a chosen people, a royal priesthood, a holy nation, a people belonging to God, that you may declare the praises of him who called you out of darkness into his wonderful light" (1 Pet. 2:9).

That too-good-to-be-true news renews our sense of wonder. Think of it: The Father makes nobodies into a chosen people. If God says we really are a royal priesthood, a holy nation, a people belonging to God, we must be. That means every congregation has lots of reasons to praise God.

Peter says believers are no longer ordinary folks. God has made us different and alive and new, so we have incredible reasons to praise Him. Every church needs more praise to God for whom He is helping them become.

Thousands of churches could be revolutionized in a week if they began to practice the motto, "Praise changes things." Or maybe the motto should be adjusted a bit, "Praise changes people who praise God." Rejoice in the wonders of God's grace that surround you in your congregation.

WHEN IS REVIVAL NEEDED?

Charles G. Finney offered a list to determine when a church needs a revival. The list from his revival lectures is timeless. He believed revivals were needed when these conditions prevailed.

- Lack of love: "When there is a lack of brotherly love and Christian confidence among professors of religion, then revival is needed."
- Disunity and division: "When there are dissensions and jealousies and evil speakings among professors of religion, then revival is needed."
- Worldliness: "When there is a worldly spirit in the church, then revival is needed."
- Sin in the church: "When the church finds its members falling into gross and scandalous sins, then revival is needed."

- Controversy and disagreement: "When there is a spirit of controversy in the church, then revival is needed."
- Wickedness controls society: "When the wicked triumph over
the churches and revile them, then revival is needed."
- Sinners are careless: "When sinners are careless and stupid,
then revival is needed."[6]

Genuine Revivals Start with Prayer
Seldom have great spiritual awakenings come to pastors, churches or
countries without intercessory prayer. John Hyde, a praying missionary,
before an awakening in India near the turn of this century, asked
Christians these questions to stimulate faithfulness in prayer for revival:

- Are you praying for quickening in your own life, in the life of
your fellow workers and in the church?
- Are you longing for greater power of the Holy Spirit in your
life and work, and are you convinced you cannot go on without this power?
- Will you pray that you may not be ashamed of Jesus?
- Do you believe that prayer is the great means for securing this
spiritual awakening?
- Will you set apart one-half hour each day as soon after noon
as possible to pray for this awakening, and are you willing to
pray till the awakening comes?[7]

REVIVAL REVOLUTIONIZES A CHURCH

Real revival restores an individual and a church to spiritual health and
well-being. For an individual, genuine revival enables him to live out his
faith in the daily details of life.

Such a renewal brings a church from subnormal, barely-making-it
Christianity to a supernatural empowerment, a refreshing, a renewal, a
sense of anointing and a growing awareness that the Church is a unique
organization owned and energized by God.

It stirs a congregation and challenges us and empowers us to live out the radical demands of Christianity in every phase of life inside and outside the church.

Spiritual Normalcy Is Restored

The main purpose of renewal and revival is not to produce supersaints or souped-up churches, although that sometimes occurs. Revival more often directs a church to its original purposes, making it more wholesome, healthy and robust or even redemptive. After restitution, forgiveness and reordering of priorities are experienced by a church, renewal and revival help believers sharpen their commitments to the church's unique roles and functions of prayer, worship, witness and service. Spiritual normalcy then returns so that a church is more than a feeble imitation of a garden club, a service club or a well-intentioned welfare organization.

Recently, a Southern California pastor shared a story of his personal journey of faith. He told about joyous renewal in the congregation he serves and expressed the belief that pastoral renewal and congregational revitalization grow in the same spiritual soil. He believes renewal in one person encourages renewal in the other.

Revival made incredible changes in his church. Early prayer meetings following the Korean pattern of morning prayer replaced a cluttered whirl of purposeless activities. His entire church is permeated with evidence of answered prayer. A new love for Scripture moves like wildfire through the fellowship so people, wherever they gather, apply the meaning of the Bible to contemporary life. A changed, energetic worship atmosphere is so common that parishioners often sing with meaning, "Surely the presence of the Lord is in this place." The pastor's sermons have a new passion and vitality.

No one can explain the amazing change because the church has the same preacher, the same songs, the same meeting time, the same worshipers and the same sanctuary. Holy living has become the routine practice of many people in the church. The pastor suggested, "My people often say the Early Church must have been a lot like the present environment in our church."

Extraordinary Prayer Is Activated

Evangelists and devotional writers are not agreed on whether prayer brings renewal or whether renewal engenders new power in prayer. It is like the chicken or the egg question. Either way, genuine revival always brings with it a component of extraordinary prayer.

It is a supernatural and satisfying kind of prayer in which the believer approaches God with a sense of humility and urgency. He stays until he knows he has communicated with God. Then he departs fully aware of having an audience with the King of the universe. It is the closest of all possible contacts with God.

Prayer is among the most popular discussion topics in church circles. We talk about prayer. We read books about prayer. We preach about prayer. We teach about prayer.

Meanwhile, it seems that the Church does not pray much. Now, the Church needs a bold urgency and fresh fervency in prayer until we know the answer is on the way because the Lord has heard us pray. It is still true, and God will continue to respond because, "The prayer of a righteous man is powerful and effective" (Jas. 5:16). Magnificent answers to critical needs for renewal come when believers really pray.

Sin Feared as a Spiritual Cancer

Revival forces a person to face sin and its incredibly damaging consequences. Sin, like cancer, requires radical surgery if a person or church is to experience spiritual health. But worse than the dreaded effects of cancer on a human being is the not-so-obvious damage that individual sins have on a congregation. The outcome impacts a church, sometimes hindering its ministry for generations. Sin is serious business that must be acknowledged, forgiven and forsaken.

Although it may not make us comfortable to think about it, many churches are crippled, anemic, handicapped, feeble and too weak for spiritual warfare because of known and unknown, inner and outer, respectable and vile sin in their fellowship. Sometimes even in the ministry.

The remedies are the same as they have always been: intercessory prayer by everyone who cares about the spiritual well-being of the church, anointed preaching on the subject that is clearly based on

Scripture and an atmosphere of deliverance in the church where recent converts are encouraged to freely tell of their transformations from the sins of their past.

Miracles Are Experienced
Many debates among ministers and scholars center around the meaning of the term "signs and wonders." Some consider signs and wonders as flamboyant, absolutely unexplainable events, while others believe that the days of miracles ended with the apostles. Sincere Christ followers can be found on both sides of the issue.

Wherever you stand in the debate, it is time to admit that the contemporary Church needs more of the supernatural and miraculous. More ministers need to put themselves in places of courageous commitment

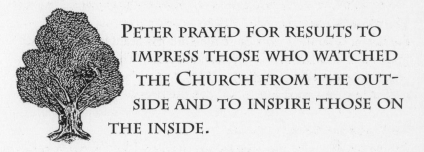

PETER PRAYED FOR RESULTS TO IMPRESS THOSE WHO WATCHED THE CHURCH FROM THE OUTSIDE AND TO INSPIRE THOSE ON THE INSIDE.

that are so demanding and so near the cutting edge that it requires God's supernatural enablement to survive or thrive.

A veteran pastor remarked recently, "Don't expect a miracle until you have gone way beyond your own resources. God doesn't waste the supernatural on what you can do on your own."

Peter, the coward before Pentecost, did this in the Early Church. In Acts 4:29,30, Peter's (and the Church's) prayer for "signs and wonders" asks God for boldness to speak convincingly before Herod and Pontius Pilate and for supernatural results in the Early Church.

Peter received boldness and results. He wanted the Early Church to be so unique and so remarkable that no one could doubt it was an instrument of God. He prayed for results to impress those who watched the

Church from the outside and to inspire those on the inside.

God answered Peter's prayer. The Bible says the place was shaken. They were filled with the Holy Spirit. They spoke the Word of God boldly. They were united. They shared everything they had, including their material possessions. They testified with great power of the Resurrection. They fed the needy. They sold their land for the cause of Christ, and all of them received much grace.

When you consider what the Church would have been without this miraculous answer to prayer, Acts 4:32-35 is a model of God giving a church exactly what it needed, more than it expected and more than members of the congregation thought they needed. It started when Peter prayed.

Results will be like that in our revivals. God will give us what we need. The work of God in the human heart and in the Church may not always be spectacular, but it will be supernatural.

National TV recently reported a story about a young Christian mother who refused to have a C-section performed because her unborn child was in medical trouble. She eventually delivered a healthy son naturally. Cynical media representatives did not know what to say, while many people accurately called it a miracle. We love the unusual and spectacular in the Church, but God also has many nonsensational miracles He wants to give every pastor and every church.

The Supernatural Continues Today

What about those close-at-hand and less sensational miracles that seldom are noticed? Here are a few that changed someone's world, but no one reported them to the press.

• Recently, a Bible college student's family in our town received $100 in the mail from an unexpected source on the day their cupboards were empty.

• A few months ago, a rebellious teenager who had been living on the streets called her Christian parents and asked to come home after being led to Christ by a street preacher.

• A short while ago, a group of laypersons confronted a church controller and told him they were tired of him dominating the church, forcing pastors' resignations and giving the church a bad name in the community. The controller left in a mad huff. Now in sweet fellowship, the lay leaders have concluded they will no longer be ruled by one person. The parting was a miracle that produced unity and peace.

• A few months ago, a minister who falsely accused a brother minister of stealing money from the church called to try to make things right. Although damages to the accused's reputation can never be fully restored, healing has started.

• Five years ago, a key layman in a middle-size church was gloriously called to the Christian ministry at age 35. His wife, unwilling to give up her home and security, openly opposed the idea. Wisely, the man simply said, "I won't make efforts to prepare until you agree wholeheartedly." He loved her, never badgered her, waiting for God's timing. God did a wonderful work in her heart and they are now students at a seminary.

Contemporary pastors need to pray Peter's prayer for their ministry setting. Who knows what God wants to do for you where you are. It might not be spectacular, but it could be supernatural.

What might happen if contemporary congregations received and used what God gave to the Church in Acts 4:32-35? Consider the remarkable possibilities for renewal in our time. They preached with supernatural power, they were filled with the Holy Spirit, they were committed to a common cause, they testified to the resurrection of Jesus, they had great grace, they gave up their security and greed by selling land and they cared for the needy. Sounds like the supernatural power of God working in a local congregation, doesn't it?

Love Becomes Magnetic

When a revival of love occurs in a church, people treat each other as they would treat Christ. The golden rule becomes spontaneous. Differences are confessed, splintered relations are repaired and restitutions are made.

Forgiveness is requested and granted. One person says, "I'm sorry" while another says, "It's okay; I should have grown past our disagreement months ago."

The glorious gift of hospitality gets dusted off. They baby-sit for each other. They became surrogate grandparents to children and love their young parents. They begin praying for each other and with each other. Love flows like a quiet river into every cranny of the church, so everyone sings better, smiles more and criticizes less.

Like a holy epidemic, renewed love at church automatically spreads outside to offices, factories, gas stations, convenience stores, schools, Fortune 500 companies—wherever Christ lovers find themselves. Holy love flowing through the people of God to the unsaved is a powerful force for evangelism. Even though spiritually needy people may not be scolded out of their sins or reasoned into the Kingdom, they can often be loved to Jesus.

In this renewal of love, a believer's witnessing becomes delightful and natural. It shows on the tennis court, on the golf course, in shopping malls, in family rooms, in PTA meetings and anywhere else we meet someone who needs the Savior. Outsiders who feel that love want to attend the church. And they often come again and again to experience the love of Christ flowing through a Christ-exalting church.

It's Time to Light Revival Fires

While pleading for revival, Charles Spurgeon challenged laypeople to stop complaining about their pastors and to stop finding fault with their churches.

He challenged laity to cry out in intercessory prayer, "O Lord, revive thy work in me!" He told laity, "You don't need a new preacher, another kind of worship, another type of preaching, new ways of doing things or even new people. You need life in what you have."[8]

Pastors need to hear a comparable message. This might be the time to get past the common and destructive "if only we had" syndrome. I've said it often and heard it many times in many places. Oh, if only we had another building. Oh, if only we had more trained laypersons. Oh, if only we had more money. Oh, if only we had a higher class of people. Oh, if only we had more commitment among the laity. Oh, if only we had a different style of worship. Oh, if only we had better or different music. Oh, if only my spouse were more involved. Oh, if only we had more Bible teachers. Oh, if only we had more social standing in the community. Oh, if only we had....

Spurgeon prescribes a cure for our "if only we had" debilitating virus. With a passionate heart burden he says, "If you want to move a train, you don't need a new engine, or even ten engines—you need to light a fire and get the steam up in the engine you now have."[9]

Spurgeon continues, "It is not a new person or a new plan, but the life of God in them that the church needs. Let us ask God for it! Perhaps He is ready to shake the world at its very foundations. Perhaps even now He is about to pour forth a mighty influence upon His people which shall make the church in this age as vital as it ever was in any age that has passed."[10]

Let's light the fire and get up steam in the engines we already have and let's pray, "O Lord, revive Thy work in me!"

A SPIRITUALLY RENEWED PASTOR

The following testimony must have been written by a renewed pastor—the kind the Church and the world need now. I regret the source is unknown to me.

A Christian leader saw it on the wall of a pastor's home in rural Africa. I have a copy from a radio preacher dated 1981, and a Bible college student found it in the notes of a pastor who has been with the Lord for several years. At any rate, it needs a wide reading and a wider replication in contemporary pastors. My appreciation and thanks to the unknown author.

I am a part of the "fellowship of the unashamed." I have Holy Spirit power. The dye has been cast. I've stepped over the line. The decision has been made. I am a disciple of His. I won't look back, let up, slow down, back away or be still. My past is redeemed, my present makes sense and my future is secure. I am finished and done with low living, sight walking, small planning, smooth knees, colorless dreams, tame visions, mundane talking, chincy giving and dwarfed goals!

I no longer need pre-eminence, prosperity, position, promotions, plaudits or popularity. I don't have to be right, first, tops, recognized, praised, regarded or rewarded. I now live by Presence, lean by faith, love by patience, lift by prayer and labor by power.

My face is set, my gait is fast, my goal is heaven, my road is narrow, my way is rough, my companions few, my Guide reliable, my mission clear. I cannot be bought, compromised, detoured, lured away, turned back, diluted or delayed. I will not flinch in the face of sacrifice, hesitate in the presence of adversity, negotiate at the table of the enemy, ponder at the pool of popularity or meander in the maze of mediocrity.

I won't give up, shut up, let up or burn up till I've preached up, prayed up, paid up, stored up and stayed up for the cause of Christ.

I am a disciple of Jesus. I must go till He comes, give till I drop and preach till everyone knows.

And when He comes to get His own, He'll have no problems recognizing me...my colors will be clear.

That makes it clear, doesn't it?

CONTEMPORARY CHALLENGE
GENUINE REVIVAL MUST START
WITH THE PASTOR

- Revival begins with a holy dissatisfaction.
- Revival can be a user-friendly word.
- The church is crippled with worldliness.
- Revival starts with prayer.
- Revival requires humility and repentance.
- Revival brings a willingness to change.
- Revival restores love in a church.

I ask no dream, no prophet's ecstasies
No sudden rending of the veil of clay
No angel visitant, no opening skies
But take the dimness of my soul away.
—Hymn by George Croly, 1854, as quoted by Tony
Campolo[11]

Notes
1. Bessie Porter Head, "O Breath of Life," *Sing to the Lord*, p. 305. Public domain.
2. Bill Bright, Editor, *The Greatest Lesson I've Ever Learned* (San Bernardino, CA: Here's Life Publishers, 1991), p. 177.
3. Richard J. Foster and James Bryan Smith, Editors, *Devotional Classics* (San Francisco, HarperSanFrancisco, 1993), p. 334.

4. *Day by Day* (Grand Rapids, MI: Baker Book House, 1953), p. 16.
5. Foster and Smith, *Devotional Classics*, p. 332.
6. Charles G. Finney, *Revival Lectures* (Grand Rapids, MI: Fleming H. Revell, 1979), p. 17-19.
7. Quote from a letter to Focus on the Family, Jan. 12, 1994.
8. Foster and Smith, *Devotional Classics*, p. 335.
9. Ibid.
10. Ibid.
11. Tony Campolo, *Wake Up America!* (San Francisco: HarperSanFrancisco, 1991), p. 179.

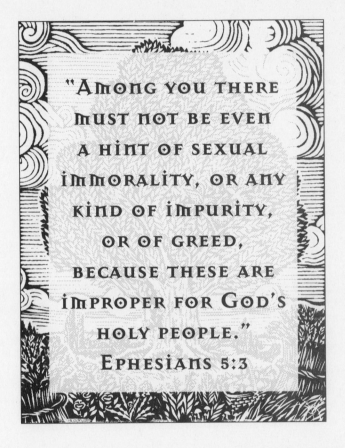

"Among you there must not be even a hint of sexual immorality, or any kind of impurity, or of greed, because these are improper for God's holy people."
Ephesians 5:3

10

Living
Above
Reproach

Holy Father, empower me for ministry
to be authentic in every act;
holy in every intention;
pure in every relationship;
genuine in every word;
and devoted in every expression of worship.
Amen.

THE QUESTION OF CREDIBILITY

Now the overseer must be above reproach, the husband of but one wife, temperate, self-controlled, respectable, hospitable, able to teach, not given to drunkenness, not violent but gentle, not quarrelsome, not a lover of money (1 Tim. 3:2,3).

In theory, all pastors would measure up to these standards Paul set for Timothy.

In practice, pastors are under siege, doing battle with a number of temptations that not only test their credibility, but also can dilute, even destroy, their ministry.

Mass media have focused on the sexual sin of several prominent ministers during the past decade. The problem, however, is not confined to celebrity status or to sexual sins. Pastors in churches large and small are subject to a vast array of temptations inherent in their profession.

Built-in temptations make pastors easy prey for ethical downfalls. Loneliness, for example, agitates vulnerability. A 1991 survey of pastors who responded to the poll said they did not have anyone they consider a close friend.[1]

Pressures on clergy marriages also cause problems. One survey of pastors shows that 33 percent were dissatisfied with the level of intimacy in their marriages, 6 percent of those spouses were dissatisfied and 19 percent have had inappropriate sexual contact with a person other than their spouse.[2] All of this was blamed on stress caused by ministry.

The absence of an accountability system may contribute to these and to other problems of temptation. Spiritual lone rangers need trusted friends to ride beside them.

Ironically, although pastors may feel alone today, they also often find that their parishioners and society have placed them on super-human perches. They are considered winners if their churches enjoy spiritual vitality and growth. They are thought of as losers if they fail to exude enthusiasm and to muster more members. Meeting the needs of other people may sap pastors of inner resources and may create a spiritual drought. On occasion, they may feel betrayed by the people they serve. Questions of how to treat family and what constitutes "free" time also test the credibility of those called to oversee ministry.

Granted, being aware of such situations does not absolve a pastor from responsibility for moral breakdowns. The temptations suggest, however, that pastors should build high hedges in their day-to-day ministry to help stop the moral hemorrhaging that saps the lifeblood from Christ's redemptive work.

PLANTING HEDGES

The idea for planting hedges to help pastors live above reproach comes from Jerry B. Jenkins's book *Loving Your Marriage Enough to Protect It*. His following suggestion helps immensely: "One of the major causes of marital breakups in the Christian community is the lack of protective hedges that spouses should plant around their marriages, their heads, their hearts, their eyes, and their hands."[3] Anyone with a little effort can build hedges and protective guardrails around his ministry.

Hedge 1: Ask for Help
Good, biblically based help for ailing relationships and sexual temptations can be found in many places these days. Parachurch ministries are coming alongside the churches with help, too. Christian counseling services are more available than ever before. Trustworthy and well-trained fellow pastors also are often willing to listen and to help you work through most problems. Some denominations are adding counseling services.

Get help when you have a problem. A pastor phoned Focus on the Family recently and almost shouted, "Somebody's gotta help. I'm about to fall. Do something. I'm involved in an emotional affair that is moving quickly toward sexual intimacy. I didn't think it would go this far. I am frightened by how much I want to continue."

The pastor received help in sorting through the issues and offers for clergy counseling near him. But all the help in the world is of no avail if you do not use it in a time of need. Prevention, soul care and early treatment efforts are needed.

Hedge 2: Live by a Code of Integrity
This hedge must be planted and cultivated and watered so it grows high enough to protect you from yourself. Then the downward slide as outlined in James 1:13-16, which moves from conception to birth of sin, is halted.

Developing a personal code of integrity starts when you commit yourself to self-imposed guidelines that provide you with a sense of moral

control of your life. Such an effort settles in your will how you will react
when temptations come. Then, when the tests come, as they will, there
will be no need to reconsider, negotiate or fantasize about giving in.
Such a code builds holy conduct into the fiber of your life before the
temptation appears.

Such guidelines are not so much to protect your public persona, to
reassure your spouse, to impress your children or to convince your
church. Although it may accomplish all of this, and more, it is a commitment to yourself and to God that you will be what you say you are.

It is the dynamics that shape your thought and behavior and make
people say of an accused pastor, "His high standards of behavior prevent
him from such conduct. He is incapable of what you say."

A personal code of integrity might be developed by personalizing and
contemporizing rules John Wesley used in the early days of Methodism.
The process works well for individuals, although Wesley used them to
establish converts in a group atmosphere of active faith and personal
accountability. Five searching questions were asked in the class meetings:

- What known sins have you committed since our last meeting?
- What temptations have you met with?
- How were you delivered?
- What have you thought, said or done of which you doubt
  whether it be sin or not?
- Have you nothing you desire to keep secret?

Another more contemporary-sounding set of guidelines comes from
Charles Swindoll. He used these rules with his staff, for himself and often
shares them in pastoral conferences:

- Have you been with a woman anywhere this past week that
  might be seen as compromising?
- Have any of your financial dealings lacked integrity?
- Have you exposed yourself to any sexually explicit material?
- Have you spent adequate time in Bible study and prayer?
- Have you given priority time to your family?

- Have you fulfilled the mandates of your calling?
- Have you just lied to me?[4]

Another set of self-imposed rules to build a strong hedge around a good marriage was crafted by Jerry B. Jenkins in a *Moody* magazine article. He suggested these safeguards to protect himself, his wife, his family, his employer and, most of all, the reputation of Christ.

- If I need to meet or dine or travel with an unrelated woman, I make it a threesome.
- I am careful about touching. I embrace only dear friends or relatives, and only in front of others.
- I pay a woman a compliment about her clothing or her work but not about her person. I think it is different to say you have a pretty outfit than to say you are beautiful.
- I avoid flirtation or suggestive conversation even in jest.
- I remind my wife often in person and writing that I remember our wedding vows to keep only unto her for as long as we both live.
- From the time I get home from work until the children go to bed, I do no writing or office work. This gives me lots of time with the family and allows time for my wife and me to continue to court and date.[5]

Hedge 3: Cultivate a Covenant Prayer Partnership

Like everyone else, a pastor needs a covenant prayer partner to whom he gives permission to inquire about his relationship to God, his prayer life, his marriage or his commitments to his family. This relationship is a covenant between two persons of the same gender who are seeking a special release of God's power on their ministry and families.

It is important that the covenant should be an agreement for at least six months and based on mutual trust. Both persons commit to pray for each other on a regular basis, at least daily. These partners meet at least once every two weeks for a time of sharing. They also keep in touch with brief phone calls and notes in the mail that say something like, "Are you working on the issue we discussed when we were last together? Are you involved in anything that would hinder your ministry or harm your witness? Are you faithful to your family?"

In such a covenant relationship, both persons receive strength through intercessory prayer, spiritual accountability and an active commitment to help another servant of the Lord. Ask others who are trusted

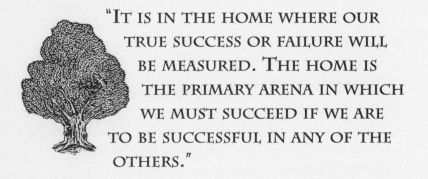

"IT IS IN THE HOME WHERE OUR TRUE SUCCESS OR FAILURE WILL BE MEASURED. THE HOME IS THE PRIMARY ARENA IN WHICH WE MUST SUCCEED IF WE ARE TO BE SUCCESSFUL IN ANY OF THE OTHERS."

prayer warriors in your church to pray for you and your family regularly. The relationship makes specific many things we plan to do for each other but never get around to doing.

The process can be uncomplicated, even simple. The key to effectiveness—it takes a great deal of trust to say to another person, "I believe in you enough that I will allow you to really know who I am in Christ."

Hedge 4: Keep the Home Fires Burning
Excellent directions for keeping your marriage satisfying when others are falling apart is given in 1 Peter 3:7-9:

> Be good husbands to your wives. Honor them, delight in them. As women they lack some of your advantages. But in the new life of God's grace, you're equals. Treat your wives, then, as equals so your prayers don't run aground. Summing up: Be agreeable, be sympathetic, be loving, be compassionate, be

humble. That goes for all of you, no exceptions. No retaliation. No sharp-tongued sarcasm. Instead, bless—that's your job to bless. You'll be a blessing and also receive a blessing.[6]

A satisfying marriage is a pastor's best insurance for sexual purity. The advice of Steve Diggs, chairman of a Nashville advertising agency, to Christian businessmen also applies to pastors: "It is in the home where our true success or failure will be measured. The home is the primary arena in which we must succeed if we are to be successful in any of the others."[7]

Although this subject is seldom discussed by convention speakers, books or tapes, letters to Focus on the Family and honest sharing conversations with ministry couples show that more attention is needed to the issues of affection, intimacy and sexual fulfillment.

Too often, clergy couples without knowing it carry unresolved intimacy frustrations from their bedrooms into their ministry. One pastor's wife said, "I carry on a cold war of pettiness and small terrorist acts because my husband flirts with a woman in church and never meets my physical needs at home."

A pastor in his late 50s wrote, "My wife and I both had brief emotional flings with people in the church. It could have been avoided so easily if we had gotten help to work through our needs for affection and caring at home. She needs more affirmation and affection from me and I need more sexual gratification from her."

He continued, "The sad part is that with a little effort we could be more for each other than anybody outside our relationship. We're working on that and our marriage is a whole lot better."

We hope these letters represent a minority. To prevent such problems, however, would require an increased concern for the needs of each spouse. Sexual frequency or technique are not as important as mutual satisfaction and an eager willingness to please each other.

Every couple could use Dr. Willard F. Harley Jr.'s summary statement in his book *His Needs, Her Needs* to open a helpful discussion of the subject: "When it comes to sex and affection, you can't have one without the other."[8]

Many ministry couples enrich their marriage by drawing up a covenant commitment. No outside list can work as well as one you have discussed and promised to each other. Here's a sample list that two mature Christian partners designed for establishing and maintaining a healthy marriage:

- God will always be the honored guest in our home.
- We work as a team in ministry.
- We are committed to each other for life.
- We will never shut the door on communications.
- We will make time to meet each other's spiritual, emotional and sexual needs.
- We will encourage each other to develop our individual gifts.

Hedge 5: Learn from Another's Failures

Too often we see other ministers fail, and we automatically assume we are incapable of such a fate. Even though we believe that we would not make the same mistake, significant lessons are to be learned. Who knows how sinful or stupid or downright silly we might be if the wrong temptations came along, as they so often do.

Listen to the pain in the following true story. An unnamed pastor asked us to share this series of events from his own ministry:

"Pastors, hear my story.

"Today, I am looking for a job, daily scouring the newspaper, sending out resumes and waiting for phone calls. A few months ago, I felt securely placed in a new church, so much so that we even purchased a house, thinking that we'd spend many years ministering there. It was not a down time. I loved my people. The church was growing. I had a good relationship with my leadership group and with members of the congregation.

"This all began to come apart when a counseling situation became a 'gripping relationship.'

"In my case, as the counseling situation began to grip me and get out of control, through prayer, common sense, a love for my wife and family, and a love for the church and its ministry, I knew that I had to do something drastic. I knew that this bad situation would only get worse if I didn't stop it quickly and decisively. It could ultimately lead to the destruction of two families, a church and my ministry.

"Up until this time, on two occasions the counselee and myself had agreed together that we could go no further. God could not honor what was happening. But we happened to get into several kinds of situations alone again. Many of these situations were not planned. The fire continued to blaze.

"I began to acknowledge to myself the possibility of a sexual relationship. I was afraid, afraid of my own feelings, afraid to tell someone, afraid not to tell someone and get accountability, and afraid of what would happen if I did tell.

"When I considered all the angles and prayed beyond my emotions, I felt led to call the area supervisor of my denomination to tell him that I was in trouble and to risk whatever the end result would be. I really didn't think my world would fall apart, and I really did desire to be right with God and right with people.

"I looked at the phone for about an hour, dialing all the numbers but the last and stopping. Suddenly I dialed all the numbers, and he answered on the first ring. Of all times, this time the secretary didn't answer! 'Dr._____, this is_____. This is not a normal call. I'm in trouble.'

"Nervously, I went on with my story.

"His advice was to tell my wife. Maybe we could keep the whole thing within the circle of the two couples and go on with what appeared to be a profitable ministry. That night I told my wife. That night the 'other' woman told her husband. I'll never forget that night. All hell seemed to break loose. It was clear that this was not going to be contained between the two couples.

"The previous Sunday was the last Sunday I spoke in that pulpit except for my resignation.

"I shared with my board honestly and with a repentant heart. I did all I knew to do. They accepted my apology and believed I was right with God but felt that my ability to minister there was diminished. Some said they still loved me but to them something was now missing. They could never see me as their pastor again. My heart was broken. I loved these people.

"The church and my superiors have treated me fairly. I still hold my ordination certificate with good standing in my denomination, but I am wounded and shy about rushing into another pastoral assignment.

"The denomination offered counseling. It has been good because some things that have never been dealt with in our marriage (and maybe never would have been dealt with) have been brought to light. Issues came from my wife and myself.

"As I look at all that has happened in recent months, I feel a loss and lack of direction since it seems I must change occupations.

"Since I faced down temptation without sin, I wonder about the ability of the church and people to be redemptive. I question the rightness of being cut off from all our Christian friends in our town at this troubled time. At times, I question God and wonder why we must face such financial hardships and loss of self-esteem when at a time of extreme temptation I did what I felt was right.

"Perhaps some good can come out of this situation if I can share with fellow pastors how I believe the Lord is showing me how this troubling situation could have been avoided. Maybe my story can help some pastor avoid ruin and realize how high the stakes really are. Maybe some pastor will realize that we, as ministers of the gospel, are on a pedestal in the minds of the people and, therefore, are judged by a different standard. Maybe someone who hasn't, will realize the very appearance of evil must be avoided.

"I offer the following thoughts for my fellow pastors:

"*The stakes are high.* Consider the high price of any inappropriate action. In our day, many are losing their ministries purely on the basis of suggestion or accusation.

"People in the church don't know how to handle trying to be redemptive, especially if they are faced with two families from two sides of the same situation. People on the outside of the church are suspicious and untrusting of the church and its leaders, looking for any flaw or failure in it or its leaders. People on both sides are often looking for someone to sue.

"*Consider not counseling members of the opposite sex alone.* If it must be done, structure as much accountability in your life as possible. Have not just one accountability partner, but three or more if necessary. I had two. With one partner it was becoming hard to get together and our schedules wouldn't mesh. With the other, we had been talking about it but we never sat down to ask the tough questions.

"You might consider these options. Refer counseling of the opposite sex to a person of the same sex. Counsel with your spouse present. If you have an associate, counsel together in some cases or plan occasions where you alternate with the associate. Report weekly to someone and have them ask tough questions like, 'How is your thought life?' and 'Is there anyone outside of your marriage that you have been sexually attracted to this week?' And, if yes, 'What are you going to do about it?'

"Consider a buddy system for counseling. Have the counselee come to the sessions with a friend you can both trust if the spouse cannot be involved. Stick to the subject in counseling.

"*Don't fool yourself into thinking you are too strong to be tempted.* Nothing is foolproof. You have to make your safeguards work. Don't think you can manage tempting situations. In my case, I knew the counselee had been molested. I was aware this offered a greater likelihood of one who had that background 'acting out' sexually. I knew she might transfer my role as a caring counselor to that of a lover. Just because I knew it, I thought that I could manage it. Remember, the times you believe you will stand are the times you are likely to fall.

"*Don't swap stories when counseling.* Swapping stories is a means of creating a bond. It takes away from the professionalism of the situation and tends to make you 'pals.' Focus on the counselee's situation in the light of the Word of God. Keep yourself a professional counselor in the eyes of the counselee. Steer away from answering questions like 'How is it at your house or in your marriage?'

"*Don't take nonverbal signs lightly.* They usually precede unwholesome involvement. Some of these are lingering looks or an appreciative hug at the end of the session. Often 'accidentally-on-purpose' body contact takes place. Some counselors start to receive little gifts of appreciation like cookies and coffee or a spoken desire to be together. Be careful if you find yourself calling on the phone just to talk without a real reason.

"*Get accountability.* Speak loudly, if you must. Speak loudly, clearly, quickly and to someone who matters. Even though my world seems to have fallen apart and right now I am not in the pulpit anymore, I don't regret my phone call to my church superior. He has been gracious and loving.

"But there is a greater reason why I am glad I called him. See, I have a little boy. He's two. The other day I was headed out of the house with a briefcase in each hand, as I have done often lately. I didn't know it, but he was behind me following me to the door. He had a lunch box in one hand and a small plastic file in the other. He was heading into the world to do what his dad does.

"He deserves to have a godly father and mother bonded together,

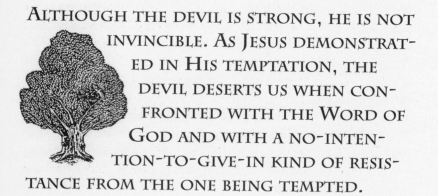

ALTHOUGH THE DEVIL IS STRONG, HE IS NOT INVINCIBLE. AS JESUS DEMONSTRAT-ED IN HIS TEMPTATION, THE DEVIL DESERTS US WHEN CON-FRONTED WITH THE WORD OF GOD AND WITH A NO-INTEN-TION-TO-GIVE-IN KIND OF RESIS-TANCE FROM THE ONE BEING TEMPTED.

rightly relating to each other with Christ in their hearts to lead him in a fallen world. I am so glad I resisted temptation and called for help so I didn't mess up his life and his mother's. Preserving your marriage and your family is worth whatever price it costs.

"*Establish safeguards before you need them.* The decisions about how you will counsel need to be made before you get into the counseling relationship. In many cases, if you have to ask, 'Is this going too far?' it has and it will be hard to turn back.

"I am trusting two promises these days: 'A broken and contrite heart, O God, you will not despise' (Ps. 51:17) and 'The Lord upholds all those who fall and lifts up all who are bowed down. The eyes of all look to you, and you give them their food at the proper time' (Ps. 145:14,15)."

Hedge 6: Maintain Your Resistance
James 4:7 tells us to resist the devil and he will flee from you. In the bib-

lical context around that verse, James tells us that God gives grace to the humble (see v. 6). Then, the apostle instructs us to submit to God (see v. 7). He assures us that if we draw near to God, He will draw near to us (see v. 8). Two verses later, we are told to humble ourselves before God and He will lift us up (see v. 10). Keeping close company with the Father keeps up resistance.

When the pastor keeps his spiritual resistance high, the devil cannot overcome him (see 1 John 5:18). Although the devil is strong, he is not invincible. As Jesus demonstrated in His temptation, the devil deserts us when confronted with the Word of God and with a no-intention-to-give-in kind of resistance from the one being tempted (see Matt. 4:1-11).

To keep spiritually healthy requires us to keep our exposure to the viruses and germs of sin to a minimum. Keep your distance from the sources of infection. Watch your company. Monitor what you view on TV according to the values of Jesus. And watch what you read.

When temptation comes, go to the Word of God to renew your resistance. If you're married, ask your spouse to pray for you, and if you have an accountability person or system, ask for help.

Hedge 7: Real Men Don't Have Affairs

This hedge is based on an essay written by Steve Farrar in the book *What Makes a Man*, sponsored by Promise Keepers. The truth, however, is as old as the Word of God. He-men in ministry are not victims of their glands nor slaves to their seductions.

They control their appetites. They allow God's power to keep them from such senseless sin and stupidity. What right-thinking man would ever choose infidelity rather than longtime affection and intimate satisfaction in marriage?

The Church must stop softening her outrage against adultery by calling it an affair. Sexual sin is heinous and devastating. Although the stigma may be acceptable in society, the sting is as painful in church and family as it always has been. It's time to shout "stop." To be heard and heeded, however, a pastor must live beyond reproach before he can denounce adultery as the deadly treason it is to the family and to the Church.

Farrar's strong paragraph needs to be personally faced by every pastor:

"When a man leaves his wife and children for another woman and acts as impulsively as an aroused junior high kid on his first date, it's not an 'affair.' It's adultery. Real men don't have affairs because real men are responsible. Real men keep their commitments, even when their person-

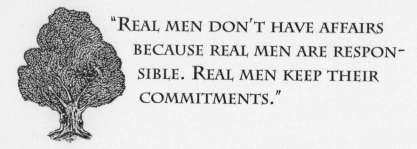

"REAL MEN DON'T HAVE AFFAIRS BECAUSE REAL MEN ARE RESPONSIBLE. REAL MEN KEEP THEIR COMMITMENTS."

al needs are not being met the way they would hope."[9] These same facts need to be preached from every pulpit.

Airtight commitments protect a pastor's marriage. This means being thoroughly Christian in thought life, conduct and influence, including emotional support of his family. As the saying goes, we must "own our lives." Thus, a pastor must be vigilant to monitor his behavior and continually to realign himself to the purposes of God. The goal is pure motives and holy character.

Hedge 8: Strive to Maintain Balance

Surveys show a direct correlation between moral failure and fatiguing burnout. After outlining the countless roles performed by an average pastor, psychologist Dr. James C. Dobson warned in a radio broadcast, "The pastorate is built for burnout, it's built for exhaustion and it's built for trouble."

He is right. Fatigue, burnout and frustration in ministry all lead to make a pastor vulnerable to fall prey to moral lapses. The guard goes down when a pastor is fatigued, works too many hours, feels sorry for himself, wonders if his work is worthwhile or quits praying.

Because the role expectations for pastors are unlikely to change in church and society in any drastic way, pastors must practice balance for themselves. Here are several useful ideas from several sources:

Office hours:
Keep regular office hours so the work routines and time at home are predictable. When conflicts arise, solve the crisis and change the schedule so your spouse or children are not cheated of your time and attention.

Soul care:
Plan specific times for personal soul care. It is the most important thing you can do for your community.

Work commitments:
Arrange your schedule so you do not give more hours to your ministry than the most active layperson gives to the church plus his job. Thus, if the active layperson invests 20 hours a week to the church plus working a 40-hour job, limit yourself to that same time commitment. To do less will encourage the laity to think you are not doing your job, so they will leave things undone, expecting you to do them.

Family:
Schedule time with your family just like any other priority item in ministry. Establish a date night each week with your spouse and schedule individual time weekly with each child. Years pass at breakneck speed with the children, and you can miss a lot before you know it.

Priorities:
Allow for shifting priorities in your schedule. Absolutely fixed priorities create major conflicts. Try priorities that move according to need. Some pastors keep one day a week open just for the purpose of being able to shift demands. Of course, a pastor always keeps God in first place. There are times, however, when a big chunk of time needs to be given to marriage, to family or to crises in ministry.

At other times you need an entire day for yourself. Shifting priorities need not be viewed as being in competition with other components of ministry. Sometimes tapping into the power of your family to strengthen, revitalize and heal your battered emotions and weary soul is the biggest favor you can do for your ministry.

Balancing ministry is a lifelong quest. Ted Engstrom, a Christian statesman, summarizes, "For a leader to excel, he must find avocations and interests in his life away from the job. He must not only provide materially for his family, but give them much of himself as well."[10]

Although balance is seldom achieved completely, the simple act of striving for balance every day and every week makes ministry more balanced than it would be with no plan.

Hedge 9: Establish Accountability

Accountability can be formal or informal, but it is essential. We all are aware of the risks because so much ministry is done alone or in one-on-one relationships, places where reliable reality checks are not often found.

Consider doing what one pastor described in a letter to H. B. at Focus on the Family:

> Last Sunday, I was reminded that my feet are still clay. Usually I find the flirtation of women other than my wife to be offensive. The last four weeks have been most demanding. I put in 76, 64, and 59 hours respectively. Needless to say, I've neglected and been neglected at home. Little time for physical or emotional intimacy. The positive feedback from my wife is low. No hostility. No arguments. No fights. But just simply the quiet of auto-pilot.
>
> Sunday an attractive young lady asked to head up VBS. She also commented on what a wonderful pastor I was. She flirts with every man in sight, and usually I find it kind of repulsive; but this Sunday, I found it exciting. Even more than that, I found she kept coming to mind, and that bothered me very much. I took time Tuesday to make myself accountable to three people—to two fellow pastors and to my wife.
>
> To the pastors, I confessed openly and asked them to hold me accountable. They will call me at unexpected times every week and ask the hard questions.
>
> Step 1: I took my wife into the picture, and I am glad. We went to lunch and talked for a long time. She had been experiencing similar things in our relationship, and we decided improvements have to be made. Think of how much joy we will find in a date every week, no matter what.

Step 2: put a 60-hour limit on my work week. Step 3 is for us to have open conversations about attractions to members of the opposite sex. And step 4 was to place our young attractive VBS director under the leadership of an older elder.

It's not over and done with, but your broadcast was the thing that stimulated me to do something about this problem. Thanks. You may have saved my ministry and marriage.

Some pastors may want more precise and regularly scheduled types of accountability. For example, Chuck Colson insists that a member of his board of Prison Fellowship review his expense records, his calendar and his priorities. He says, "I make no major decision unless the circle to which I am accountable agrees unanimously."[11]

Others may need to use a group. Engstrom outlines a plan for a peer accountability group that could work well for pastors: "For eight years I have been meeting five other men for breakfast in a restaurant. It is not a prayer meeting, but we pray together. It is not a Bible study, but we refer to the Word of God together. Because of our schedules, seldom are all six of us there, but always three or four, sometimes five.

"We are accountable to each other, for we uphold each other in many ways. I am accountable to them; they are accountable to me. A leader needs to be a part of such a peer group. How often we as Christian leaders have missed this accountability factor."[12]

From the writings of John Wesley, several lists of questions are used by the Methodists to examine themselves and others. These are different from those used in the class meetings that were cited earlier in this chapter. Any of these questions might be useful in a peer accountability group:

- Is the love of God shed abroad in your heart?
- Has any sin, inward or outward, dominion over you?
- Do I really desire others to tell me what they think, fear and hear concerning me?
- Have I mentioned any failing or fault of any man when it was unnecessary to do so?
- Have I unnecessarily grieved anyone by word or deed?

- Have I desired the praise of men?
- Have I set aside some time for endeavoring after a lively sense of the sufferings of Christ and my own sins?
- Have I resumed my claim to my body, soul, friends, fame or fortune, which I have made over to God?
- Have I said anything with stern look, accent or gesture, particularly regarding religion?[13]

Hedge 10: Nurture Soul Friends

I (H. B.) often rejoice about five soul friends in my life whom I have known and cherished for years. These five would go to the mat for me, and I would do the same for them. One of them is Dr. James C. Dobson. The others are a college vice president in Boston, a pastor in San Luis Obispo, a psychologist in Phoenix and a pastor in Detroit.

I feel unbelievably blessed in these relationships with these lifelong friends who would put their life on the line for me. These relationships have developed over long years of interaction, jousting, time together and sharing honestly and openly.

We've shared pain and heartache as well as joy. We've been through rough spots in parenting and problems in marriages. One lost his wife in death. Another had children who were out of control. One had a moral breakdown.

But still there is a bond that cannot be broken. And these friends make me more real and authentic with their questions and warnings. They say, "Be real, H. B. Stop playing games, H. B. Get authentic, H. B."

And they ask, "Tell us what is really going on, H. B." We have this confidential, supporting, warning, bonding relationship that says you can count on me unconditionally. These friends sustain me and support me and make me accountable to them and finally to the Lord Jesus.

Soul friends provide invaluable inspiration, information, correction and spiritual-growth cultivation. They make me sing the old hymn with new meaning, "I would be true for there are those who trust me. I would be pure, for there are those who care."[14]

Next to pleasing the Lord Jesus, soul friends might be the strongest possible source of accountability: They trust me and they care.

HIGH HEDGES AND OPEN HEARTS

Sturdy hedges help protect our families and prevent us from doing something cheap, questionable or immoral. While we are building hedges in creative, positive and upbeat ways, we need to communicate these views and actions in positive ways. We can, for example, remind our parishioners from the pulpit "that my marriage is among the most cherished relationships in my life."

We also can demonstrate how a healthy home inspires ministry and the high regard we hold for our family. And we should live out our com-

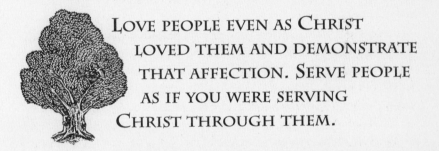

LOVE PEOPLE EVEN AS CHRIST LOVED THEM AND DEMONSTRATE THAT AFFECTION. SERVE PEOPLE AS IF YOU WERE SERVING CHRIST THROUGH THEM.

mitment to high hedges with those we love at the breakfast table, in our family discussions and in our bedrooms.

Hedges to help us live beyond reproach are proper and necessary because they help us please the Savior, authenticate our ministry in the minds of our congregation, reassure our spouses and families and generate fulfillment in ourselves.

Hedges Should Not Become Fences

A caution is worth noting. Special care must be taken in our hedge building to avoid shutting people out of our lives. Ministry, at its heart, is always relating to people in a thousand ways. Hedges need not become fences to keep us away from the people in the parish. Our hearts contain enough room to love people in our congregations while we are loving our spouses and our children.

Build the hedges high around your ministry, but do it in ways that

allow you to welcome those you meet as potential best friends. Love people even as Christ loved them and demonstrate that affection. Serve people, even unusual ones, as if you were serving Christ through them.
Building healthy hedges around your ministry makes it possible to serve
people more constructively and more joyously.

Most parishioners feel secure and trusting with a pastor who openly
speaks and demonstrates his affection for them while he is showing devotion and love for his wife and family. To be fulfilled, a pastor needs the
love of family and congregation, and he needs to love both family and
congregation.

Live Above Reproach
Living above reproach never restricts, but frees, ministry. Such a manner
of life does not make ministry harder, but makes it easier by drawing people to our authenticity. Such a manner of life does not squeeze adventure
out of ministry, but gives us a singing heart that stands without shame
before God and with no regret before the people.

Dr. Archibald D. Hart helps us see how every expression of pastoral
integrity toughens our spiritual awareness:

> A healthy concern for morality is not enough to maintain a
> ministry of integrity. Each pastor has a responsibility to devel-
> op a personal code of ethics tailored to his unique set of cir-
> cumstances.
>
> Simply wrestling with such a personal code begins to sen-
> sitize one to important issues. Over time, there begins to
> develop an "ethical sense"—a natural ability to tell if any
> action is likely to become a problem.[15]

An authentic current relationship to God is the source of pastoral
power that impacts every phase of ministry. It is the fountainhead for a
Christlike character, a joyous Christian experience, a genuine call to
ministry, a soundness of doctrine and an effectiveness of preparation.

Pastors seldom are forced to forfeit ministry because of incompetence,
but because of impurity. Holy character is the bedrock foundation of

ministry. Character made pure and empowered by God has magnetic attraction to all to whom we minister. This gives a minister sensibility, stability and stamina in a world where so much is uncertain, alienated and morally unstable.

Now, three questions need your answer.

1. If not you, who?
2. If not where you're planted, where?
3. If not now, when?[16]

CONTEMPORARY CHALLENGE
LIVING ABOVE REPROACH

- A suspicious world needs authentic ministry.
- Vocational hazards do not absolve moral breakdowns.
- Every clergy marriage needs a high hedge.
- Satisfying marriages are a resource to ministry.
- Every pastor needs a code of integrity.
- Accountability must be self-imposed.
- Soul friends encourage accountability.
- Real men don't commit adultery.

Credibility is a by-product of a Christlike character.
—Retired pastor

Notes

1. H. B. London and Neil B. Wiseman, *Pastors at Risk* (Wheaton, IL: Victor Books, 1993), p. 22.

2. "Is the Pastor's Family Safe at Home?" *Leadership*, Fall 1992, pp. 38-44.

3. Jerry B. Jenkins, *Loving Your Marriage Enough to Protect It* (Chicago: Moody Press, 1993).

4. Charles Swindoll, as quoted in *The Body: Being Light in Darkness* by Chuck Colson (Dallas, TX: WORD, Inc., 1992), p. 131.

5. Jerry B. Jenkins, *Moody*, July/August 1987, inside front cover.

6. Eugene H. Petersen, *The Message* (Colorado Springs: NavPress, 1993), p. 491.

7. Steve Diggs, *Free to Succeed* (Grand Rapids, MI: Fleming H. Revell, 1992), p. 211.

8. Willard F. Harley Jr., *His Needs, Her Needs* (Grand Rapids, MI: Fleming H. Revell, 1986), p. 124.

9. Bill McCartney, editor, *What Makes a Man?* (Colorado Springs: NavPress, 1993), p. 80.

10. Ted Engstrom, *The Makings of a Christian Leader* (Grand Rapids, MI: Zondervan Publishing, 1976), p. 117.

11. Colson, *The Body*, p. 131.

12. Engstrom, *The Makings of a Christian Leader*, p. 207.

13. Frank Bateman Stanger, *Spiritual Formation in the Local Church* (Grand Rapids, MI: Zondervan Publishing, 1989), p. 29.

14. Howard A. Walter, "I Would Be True," *Sing to the Lord* (Kansas City, MO: Lillenas, 1993), p. 493.

15. Archibald D. Hart, *Leadership*, Vol. IX, No. 2 (Spring 1988), p. 29.

16. Adapted from Stan Mooneyham, *New Every Morning*, compiled by Al Bryant (Dallas, TX: WORD, Inc., 1985), p. 149.

EPILOGUE

DON'T TRY TO DO IT ALONE

We hope you have read this far. If not, you may want to begin here. What we have shared with you represents a love letter from our hearts concerning your ministry. Together, we have labored for nearly 60 years in pastoral ministry. We know it's tough out there, and the chances of it getting much better without a genuine revival are not very good. What that means is that you, the pastors, have your work cut out for you. Yet we must constantly be reminded that the Church is His Church. He will build His Church. We must acknowledge the problems but look past the threat to the empowerment of God. We dare not deny the diagnosis but we must also apply the cure—the gospel.

Remember the promise of Jesus: "And I tell you that you are Peter, and on this rock I will build my church, and the gates of Hades will not overcome it" (Matt. 16:18).

Sometimes we think pastors and Christian leaders forget this and feel as though we must resort to theatrics and personality to make it happen. We beg you not to fall into that trap. In many ways, the Church in North America is like a struggling athletic team—we must return to fundamentals—prayer, faith, humility, repentance. Those same things that moved the Early Church out of the doldrums and into a world that watched in amazement are available to us today. Even then it will not be easy; take courage, exercise hope and redouble your efforts

We in the Church are engaged in a real battle, and at times it seems the troops are unaware of the stakes. We have grown passionless. Not so unlike the church at Ephesus, we may be in danger of losing our first love (see Rev. 2:4). At least that's what a lot of observers of church life feel. Please don't let this happen. We must regroup and press on. Remember, you're a winner on the winning team. You must never forget that.

We have attempted to say several things to you in this book that possibly bear repeating or at least a review.

God's call. You are very special. In His own wisdom, God laid His hand upon you unlike any other person in the world. He prepared you for such a time as this. "You did not choose me, but I chose you and appointed you to go and bear fruit—fruit that will last" (John 15:16).

God's heart. Like David, who was a man after God's own heart, He wants your heart to be broken by the things that break His heart. We represent a clergy that is "bottom line" motivated rather than by love for Him and His creation. We urge you to bind up some wounds, walk the back streets, put your arms around "lepers" and have a cup of coffee with some nameless, faceless people. Be Jesus to those you meet along the way and you will never be the same again!

God's place. Moses had a place. David had a place. Paul had a place. Peter had a place, and so has God prepared a place for you. We have often used a statement in this book, "Bloom where you are planted." Please do not look over God's shoulder for the next place or the next move. Look into His eyes and you will know what He wants for you, where He wants you. We sense in our interaction with pastors a restlessness. Not so unlike a person climbing the corporate ladder. We see pastors "playing" the climbing game rather than paying the price of longevity. Perhaps, like Peter, it is time to "let down your nets" (see Luke 5:4). See what miracle God has in mind for you. "No eye has seen, no ear has heard, no mind has conceived what God has prepared for those who love him" (1 Cor. 2:9).

God's gift. You are uniquely qualified for the opportunity God has allowed you. So you may not have as many gifts as the guy down the street. So what! We can become "gift greedy" if we are not careful. That's why so many of you spend so much time on your lesser gifts. This explains much of your frustration, and it could be why you are easily distracted by minor things. Spend time doing what you do best. Give it your best. Come home in the evenings with a good tiredness. It sounds trite, but we heard it somewhere: It's better to run the risk of wearing out than rusting out. Make the most of every God-given opportunity. The time is short.

God's dream. Remember the phrase we used in chapter 3? "The dream never dies, just the dreamer...the song never stops, just the singer." Well, it's true. You lose your dream, you lose your song, and you will find yourself terribly frustrated. Get in touch with His dream for you, and remember, nearly all of God's dreams seem impossible at first, but if they are His dreams for you He will make a way. The world will stomp on your flowers. It may even destroy some of them, but it can never take away the power that caused those flowers to grow in the first place. The world will play with your dreams, even cause you to wonder if it will pay to dream again. It does! We guarantee you, it will. Dream on!

The Heart of a Great Pastor has been our love letter to you. Yet, in another way, it has been a pep talk. What we hope you feel from us is support. We are in your corner. What happens to you matters to us. Call us. Write us. Pay us a visit. We may not have all the answers, but we do have a genuine desire to listen.

So—don't play the numbers game. Don't get into a ladder-climbing contest. Don't look over God's shoulder for the next move. Don't feel insignificant—ever! Bloom where you are planted. Defy the troubling reports. Stay the course. Straight ahead. Don't ever quit—dream on! Above all—keep hope alive. Endure hardship, if necessary, for the most important cause in the world.

We believe in you, and we pray that you will take all the strength you need from God for the journey. We have been doing the "pastor thing" for a long time and, in many ways, the words of an anonymous writer express our hope:

We've dreamed many dreams
    that never came true.
We've seen them vanish at dawn.
But we've realized enough
    of our dreams, thank God,
To make us want to dream on.

—H. B. and Neil